Clay

Clay

Contemporary Ceramic Artisans

Amber Creswell Bell

With 231 illustrations

Amber Creswell Bell is an arts, design and lifestyle writer, and curator. She champions emerging artists and ceramicists and is the Director of Emerging Art for Michael Reid Galleries, where she co-founded the National Emerging Art Prize in 2021. Amber is the author of *A Painted Landscape* (2018), *Still Life* (2021) and *Art Design Life* (2021), all published by Thames & Hudson.

First published in Australia in 2016 by
Thames & Hudson Australia Pty Ltd

First published in the United Kingdom in 2017 by
Thames & Hudson Ltd, 181A High Holborn, London WC1V 7QX

First published in the United States of America in 2017 by
Thames & Hudson Inc., 500 Fifth Avenue, New York, New York 10110

Reprinted 2023

Clay: Contemporary Ceramic Artisans © 2016 Thames & Hudson Australia Pty Ltd
Text © 2016 Amber Creswell Bell

Cover photography: Luisa Brimble
Design: Ngaio Parr
Editing: Tusk Studio
Proofreading: Writers Reign

The moral right of the author has been asserted.

British Library Cataloguing-in-Publication Data
A catalogue record for this book is available from the British Library

Library of Congress Control Number 2016943098

ISBN 978-0-500-50072-9

Printed and bound in China by 1010 Printing International Ltd

Be the first to know about our new releases, exclusive content and author events by visiting
thamesandhudson.com
thamesandhudsonusa.com
thamesandhudson.com.au

Contents

Foreword

Keith Brymer Jones

Ceramics has been a significant part of my life for over 40 years. In some ways it has moulded my life in the same way as I have manipulated clay on my wheel. Since leaving school at the age of 18 and going to work in a pottery as a clay boy, I have always been fascinated by making clay from the raw materials that the earth offers up to us. I am constantly amazed that a malleable material such as clay can be fired and then frozen in time. Predominantly learning my skill and discipline as a production thrower has given me an incredible daily insight into the strengths and weaknesses of clay as a medium, and therefore the possibilities of the material. The myriad of different clay bodies and combinations or recipes of the glazes, pigments and oxides are a testament to the longevity and resilience of this wonderful material that I have had the pleasure and the honour of working with all my adult life.

Clay has unique and timeless properties that lie within it. From the moment it was discovered thousands of years ago, it has shaped the way we have communicated through form and function. Not only in the practical sense, but also in an emotional one. The artistic endeavours of ceramic artisans throughout history have conveyed various messages, either by depicting stories or by way of conceptual surface design and pattern. The endless variations of this wonderful material have given us infinite possibilities in producing objects that span the aesthetic spectrum of all human desires.

To be a potter or ceramic artist, or indeed to sculpt in clay, is to be a true alchemist, literally changing the physicality of the clay one works with. From the construction to the decorating, one is dealing with the very fundamentals of chemistry. Using oxides, glaze pigments, glazes and lustres – to name but a few options open to the potter – not to mention the clay itself, means truly forming something out of fire and heat!

Within the pages of this wonderful book is an incredible spectrum of potters and contemporary ceramic artisans from around the world. It illustrates with wonderful photography the diverse techniques and styles of each potter, and explains their work ethos, their inspiration and their ability to strive and ultimately achieve their conceptual idea through the medium of clay. Each potter listed has a unique relationship with the clay, which they then illuminate through their work, whether by throwing, hand building, coiling or press moulding. Not only does this book give the reader a unique insight into the potters, but it also shows the incredibly broad spectrum of the craft and highlights beautifully the artistic nature of clay.

Enjoy ... I did!

Introduction

Why ceramics? Why now? Not since the mid-century has there been such an a clear and popular appreciation for pottery and ceramics. Studio pottery in particular – which denotes professional and amateur artists working alone, making one-off or short-run pieces – is enjoying a marked renaissance. It could be said that this current fervent public interest is part of a broader movement – a craft revival of sorts.

To the Modernists of the 20th century, 'craft' – including pottery – was anachronistic and quaint. The other camp, the craft enthusiasts, rejected the soullessness of Modernism's clean lines, clutching ever more tightly to the artisanal traditions of craftsmanship, decorative art and deference to their predecessors' techniques. After years in which studio pottery has seemingly been ignored outside a dwindling community of devotees and less often pursued as a serious profession – not least smothered by a tide of cheaply mass-produced ceramic imports – the field has recently gained a new legion of fans, collectors and makers alike traversing age, geography and demographics.

In the 21st-century landscape, where things move fast and we increasingly live in a virtual world, where everyday items are mass produced and often disposable, there has been a perceptible movement in retaliation against this life of 'haste and waste'. The ubiquity of technology has moved us to seek something other, something more 'human'. In a similar vein to the Arts and Craft movement emerging as a response to the Industrial Revolution in the 1860s, we are now answering to the current 'Digital Revolution' with a hunger for the authentic.

'Slow living' is being embraced in all its facets, encompassing a life of simplicity and less-is-more, with a shifting focus on quality of life as opposed to quantity of possessions. We are espousing organic subsistence permaculture, unprocessed and homegrown food, and slow cooking.

This new mindfulness extends to an appreciation of things that are made by hand, not in a factory, and with this comes a desire for the imperfect, the original and the unique. We are drawn to items that represent this slowness, that reflect the marks of the maker, and embody the individuality that comes with objects created by human hands.

The vehicle that so aptly and tangibly captures this notion is ceramics. Nothing so strikingly connotes this unity of human hands and earthly materials as pottery. It is almost impossible to look at an object fashioned from clay and not imagine the hands of the maker contorting around the material and giving rise to the piece's form.

Ironically, the same phenomenon that has contributed to speeding up our lives – social media – has also, in many ways, facilitated this immense

interest in the handmade. Image-sharing social networks with an inherent 'aesthetic' or 'lifestyle' bent, such as Instagram and Pinterest, have doubled their users since 2012, and many trends and tastes have been spread through the use of hashtags and the viral nature of online voyeurism. At a glance, search-friendly tags such as 'ceramics', 'pottery', 'clay' and 'handmade' have well over one million posts each – and counting.

Ceramicists now have access to these platforms to promote their work and gather fans. Simultaneously, pottery schools, workshops and courses are springing up everywhere as novices learn to throw and hand build their own dinnerware – and share their accomplishments online. Pottery schools have also indicated an increase in demand since 2012 – with many now reporting long waiting lists, moving to larger premises and buying additional kilns to satisfy demand. The emergence of boutiques and retail stores selling ceramics alongside fashion and on-trend homewares indicates that demand has far exceeded that which off-track galleries and artisanal markets can supply. Ceramics have even made it into the mainstream realm of reality television, with programs such as the BBC's *The Great Pottery Throw Down* having become popular viewing.

Stemming from the ancient use of clay to create functional objects such as bowls and jugs, ceramics has, over time, evolved to provide people with decorative pieces and, eventually, fine art. Today, ceramics covers a wide range of styles, from traditional pottery-based objects to avant-garde non-functional creations. The combinations of inspiration, materials, and methodology are infinite. It is this rich eclecticism that makes studio pottery so appealing, allowing makers to uniquely express their character through their work.

Clay: Contemporary Ceramic Artisans seeks to explore this uniqueness in a contemporary global context. It is a showcase of the new clay artisans, a snapshot, not necessarily of what is happening at a national gallery level, but rather what is happening in studios around the world. *Clay* aims to illustrate the diverse styles and output of the creatives moving in the space today – why they've chosen this path,

what their work represents, how they describe their style and influences, what they love about working with the medium, the joys and challenges. Some have been tertiary trained in ceramic arts while others have decades of studio experience – and others have changed careers entirely to follow their creative passion. Some are new to the game, but clearly have great intuition and talent.

This book does not intend to be an academic 'best of', documenting all the key ceramicists of our time, nor a technical exploration of ceramic methodology. It is a somewhat subjective curation aiming to shine light on a diverse cross-section of styles, experiences, geography and personality of the artists who have elected to work with this medium.

Through exploring the personal stories of the 53 artists interviewed in this book, it became apparent that, for all the diversity, several universal truths were emerging, running like a thread linking one story to another. It can safely be said that two influential 20th-century British studio potters – Austrian-born Dame Lucie Rie and German-born Hans Coper – are enduring

muses. It is also clear that in ceramics, disasters are inevitable and detachment is part of the maturity and evolution of a ceramics practice. Those working with clay tend to describe a mystical, meditative quality to the material, and also say that the opening of a kiln post-firing is most certainly one of the greatest joys to be had. Clay is very much recognized as a material steeped in history and tradition, and to work with such a material comes with an inherent sense of honour. To an artisan creating functional pieces out of clay, the feedback from others who love and use those pieces is immensely important. It can also be said that clay has a language of its own that cannot be expressed verbally, and terms of addiction – such as being 'hooked' – are very common. I hope that this book captures the spirit of the current clay renaissance, and all the creativity, consideration, skill, experience and talent that it represents.

Akiko Hirai Collingwood

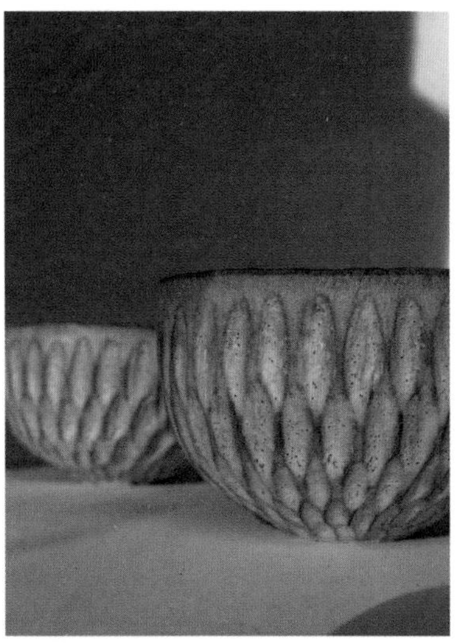

Above: Akiko's work draws on Japanese ceramic traditions.

Akiko Hirai Collingwood's passion for ceramics is connected to her hobby of writing short stories, poems and essays, which started in her adolescence. 'I was an enthusiastic reader, especially of stories that are visually descriptive. You have to read between the lines, to create the scenarios in your mind,' she says. Akiko finds that it helps to write short narratives when she's beginning new projects, and to then make her work correspond to these narratives.

Born in Japan, Akiko first came to England as a language student, to visit her sister who was living there. For a while she toyed with the idea of gaining her masters in psychology in the UK. 'While I was staying there I had an opportunity to take a short pottery course in the local college, and met a few potters working in London. I was a very keen student and some people told me to go to university to study ceramics. The idea seemed to be impossible to me as I was a beginner and had no previous experiences', she says. However, Akiko was brought up in an environment where being an artist or a potter was very much a legitimate career choice. She was inspired to apply and, fortunately for her, her university application was accepted. 'Despite having little experience, I found learning was very enjoyable. Like many Japanese I liked pottery as a viewer. Also my grandmother was a teacher of sencha tea ceremony, so ceramic teaware were familiar objects to me,' Akiko explains.

Naturally, Akiko chose to research two kinds of ceramics that are highly appreciated in Japan. The first was kohiki ware (high-fired white slipware), a rather modest kind of ceramics where the top layer is white, yet the body colour underneath shows through. The second was wood-fired stoneware, where wood ash becomes a natural glaze on the surface of pots, with the result being semi-spontaneous. 'I was attracted to the vigorous texture created by the process of firing. Realistically, wood firing seemed too challenging in an urban environment, so I decided to research the magic material "wood ash" instead,' Akiko explains.

Akiko's initial intention was to replicate the effects of these two types of ceramics. However, after numerous tests, Akiko developed

her own styles. Akiko's favourite writing subjects are the small
pleasures of everyday life — the smell of early morning air, the feeling
of discovering the white moon between trees, and the small daily
events that give you a particular sensation. 'In this same way I chose
to make domestic ware because it is constantly used and close to our
everyday life. It is not big, expressive art. That is what suits my own
aesthetics and expression,' she explains.

Akiko has a habit of leaving imperfections as a characteristic
of her work. 'Imperfection works like a metaphor, not describing
everything but leaving space for the viewer's imagination.'

The honesty of the material resonates so importantly for Akiko,
and is at the core of her practice. She relishes the simple magic that
comes from a tiny amount of impurity in the clay and the reactions
that occur in the extreme heat of the kiln. Her philosophy for working
in this medium is simply to be patient and resilient.

Above: Akiko applies ash
directly to the surface of her
Amamori Plates using a
transparent glaze.

Above: The ash used on Akiko's *Spring Plate* is made from ash tree wood from Devon.
Opposite: The *Blue Moon Jar* is reduction fired with a transparent glaze.

'Knowing materials and techniques is like increasing your vocabulary. But having a large vocabulary is only useful when you have things to say.'

Akio Nukaga

Although he graduated from Tokyo Zokei University with a major in textile design, Akio Nukaga was convinced that art and design were not actually suitable vocations for him. But given his love of making things, he was determined to be an artisan of some form. Living in Japan, where pottery is a ubiquitous presence, he soon found himself drawn onto a path in ceramics.

Once Akio had decided to pursue ceramics, he knew that it was essential to gain experience at one of Japan's many handmade pottery manufacturers, with the ultimate aim of becoming a throwing craftsperson. He finished a one-year ceramics course in Kasama, Ibaraki, and then started working for Kozan-Kiln, a long-established business with a reputation for handcrafted ceramics. 'The owner of Kozan-Kiln could make one thousand Japanese teacups in a day – and I was very eager to learn his technique! I worked for him for four years and then felt ready to start my own studio in 1993,' he says.

Akio's works are for daily use, with a deliberate effort to imbue his pieces with soul. He feels that it is important for his works to have 'warm forms', which manifest as characteristics of simplicity, naïve texture, tactile materials and a harmonization with the environment of cookery. 'I want owners of my pottery to use them for the long term, so I meticulously design my work with timeless qualities. I make yellow glazed work – a combination of black and pale yellow – and pleated work – black and white contrast, called the Shinogi technique,' he explains.

Primarily using a pottery wheel, Akio works with red clay (and occasionally porcelain clay), using slip and engobe to embellish. For his cherished traditional Shinogi work, he employs a carving technique. Akio explains that Mingei – the Japanese folk art movement developed in the late 1920s and 1930s – influences his work and style. 'I am happy to acquire mass-production techniques using a pottery wheel, perfected by predecessor potters. These techniques

Left: Akio in his studio, surrounded by examples of his work.

are my true treasure. When I worked at Kozan-Kiln, I noticed there was a slight difference among potters, even though they were meant to make the same item. Akio lives and works in an area between neighbouring pottery towns Kasama and Mashiko, where hundreds of fellow potters reside. This region is a true tourist destination for ceramic-lovers, and welcoming visitors to his studio is something that Akio relishes, 'I love making pottery and working as a potter. I like to mingle with my customers, as it inspires me to create. I consider users of my pottery as supporters and friends who can share in the same virtues of my work.'

All ceramicists know that to work with this medium requires steeling oneself against the inevitable breakages that come from working with kilns and human handling. However, for Akio the greatest heartbreak came with the huge earthquake that hit Japan in March 2011. 'I was at the Narita airport ready to fly to the USA for the opening of my private show at Heath Ceramics in California the next day. My studio was extensively damaged, and I barely made it to my show. After the catastrophe, I linked with many potters in Mashiko and the neighbouring pottery town of Kasama via social media, which provided much emotional support. It was a very difficult time.'

Akio Nukaga is now very much considered a master potter. His vases, pitchers, bowls, cups and containers merge craft with design at the highest level, with his recognizable limited palette and very sophisticated sense of scale and proportion, for which he is internationally celebrated.

Above: Akio cherishes the traditional Kasama pottery carving technique he uses for his Shinogi work.
Opposite: Akio's work using the Shinogi technique – 'pleated' clay with black and white contrast.

Above and opposite: Akio at work in his studio.

'Japan has a long history of potteries. They have been nurtured along with Japanese culture and I am touched by my predecessor potters' work.'

Alana Wilson

According to Alana Wilson, practising ceramics allows her to create pieces that interact with people's everyday lives. She means that the utilitarian aspects of ceramics help to solidify its relationship with physicality, reality and humanity in ways that she feels some mediums of contemporary art cannot. 'Much of what we know of the oldest cultures of this Earth is communicated through vessels and utilitarian objects that have withstood time. There is an extremely rich history of ceramics – different in so many cultures – that contributes to anthropology and cultural documentation as much as fine art,' she says.

Choosing not to adhere to a specific style, Alana aims instead to embed or communicate concepts in her work. Her signature pieces are light, serene and textured, making use of referential, contemporary, experimental and archaeological elements. Her hallmarks appear as forms and glazes that she repeats and develops consistently.

The bodies of Alana's vessels are created using porcelain paper clay and terracotta paper clay. She finds the structure of this clay works perfectly for her hand-building and coiling methods and that, once fired, it is much lighter, which allows her to make large pieces that take several days to construct. With her glazing process, layers of washes, slips and glaze are built up and react in the 1260°C heat of the firing. The results include textural build-up, flashing, vaporization of air-borne ingredients and a multitude of chemical changes that contribute to the final surface.

Alana's work is informed by an accumulation of many people and experiences. 'One major influence, which is not just integral to my work but forever integral to my lifestyle, is water, and also space. I grew up between Australia and New Zealand, in a family of swimmers, with my parents running a swim school. I swam competitively, so most mornings, evenings and weekends were spent in and around the pool or at the beach. This vast natural environment has been immensely influential.'

Growing up, Alana was always quite creative, predominantly in a spatial sense, with surfaces and objects in an environment, as opposed to images. This eventually led her to completing a degree in fine arts at the National Art School in Sydney. 'I did ceramics on my first day and was in love from the beginning. I finished my postgraduate studies in 2012 and have been practising since.'

Now, as a full-time artist, Alana describes the primary challenge as communicating her ideas and

Left: The bodies of Alana's vessels are made from paper clay.

work in the most succinct and truest way, at the right time and in the right place. 'Finding the right people to build working relationships with, people who share your vision, is an important aspect. In Australia, the geographical isolation can be a challenge in building an international audience and network,' she notes.

Alana concedes that the challenges — once you overcome them — ultimately lead to the positive. 'Everything else is joy! I particularly love it when I see my work has connected strongly with someone,' she says. 'I believe human connection is the most important thing in life, as well as the most rewarding, and for this to be achieved through my work is a great joy. Being able to do what I love every day is the biggest thrill I could have.'

What she loves most are the surprises inherent in her craft. 'I put something in the kiln, hope for the best and then am often pleasantly surprised by the results,' says Alana. 'There's a degree of control that you have but you can never make exactly the same thing twice. There is always variation and I like that, it means you can't be too precious or hold things too close.'

Above and opposite: Alana's aim is to create pieces that people use in their daily lives.

'The aspect of chance within a firing and the surrender to an elemental process is another joy of working in ceramics.'

Alexandra Standen

When Alexandra Standen decided to go to art school she had no notion that she would ultimately end up choosing ceramics as an art practice. It was in her first year at Sydney's National Art School in 2008 that she fell in love with the modesty of clay, and with the real beauty and authenticity of function.

Alexandra explains that after four years of studying she was fortunate to be selected by a gallery in Sydney and was able to start making a career from her art practice straight away. She entered numerous awards and art prizes that gave her the opportunity to show her work in different galleries and museums around Australia. 'From this starting point my work has matured and I continue to push myself out of my comfort zone to keep everything interesting and inspired. I have been very lucky in many ways that I can make art my full-time job. I am now also back at uni, undertaking a two-year research masters at UNSW Art & Design,' she says. 'I am looking to better understand why we collect and store certain things, and why objects of function become valuable after they have been taken out of their intended, functional environment. I think in collecting functional objects we build stories and histories into them. I love that idea. It's very romantic.'

Alexandra's work has evolved significantly over recent years. Her current work is focused on porcelain and hand building large vessels that she paints with a ceramic blue pigment – a blue that has become something of a signature in her work. She explores the possibilities of arrangement through creating collections of related forms, and examines the ideas of ritual, ordinariness, contemplation and environment. 'Central to this process is identifying and capturing an essence of life so that my work can draw breath, hold space and speak of energy and emotion; all of which is an essential part of what it means to be human. My work addresses the most primordial, historical material – clay – transforming it into a vessel, and extending this language to objects of containment and inner space.'

Alexandra hand builds forms by pinching thin coils of clay together, mainly using porcelain and clean, crisp-coloured pigment for the surface. She compresses the clay to the extent that it becomes quite delicate, firing the work to 1300°C in an electric kiln – although she is open to experimenting with different glaze technology and clay bodies. While the resulting forms are usually vessels, they often take on a sculptural nature.

Left: Alexandra displays one of her pieces.

The process-driven nature of a ceramics practice has, as Alexandra puts it, a meditative quality, which she finds enjoyable. Despite the calm atmosphere, she describes the frustrations of trying to make sense of her work. 'I sometimes struggle to see the purpose of the objects I make and I question the relevance of such a personal creation in someone else's life. This is an ongoing challenge for me. Working through experimental ideas and questioning functionality, fragility and narrative seem to be bigger challenges than moulding the clay into a pleasing object. As I work through my [masters] I find all these questions of purpose swimming around in my head and it's a little hard to separate these thoughts from an instinctual making process sometimes.'

Alexandra says that one of the true pleasures of her craft is the joy of opening a kiln full of works that have survived the firing process. She also appreciates the sense of fulfilment that comes from the positive reactions of others who use her pieces. 'I can't explain how much joy there is in an individual response to your work,' she says. 'When someone tells you that they own a piece and love it or use it daily, it gives you such an encouraging feeling.'

Listening to a talk recently by Esther Freud, who spoke about her childhood and relationships with her mother and famous artist father Lucian, left Alexandra with a thought that continues to motivate her. 'The most inspiring thing she talked about was her practice as a writer and how she built a career. She said, "You can be creative in many areas of your life, but in order to do something big, like write a book or paint a picture," – or in my case make a vessel – "you must have discipline. If you carry on and carry on, you will get somewhere eventually." So that is my advice to others; be considerate, generous and hard-working.'

CLAY

'The process of making these objects has become part of my life and I couldn't imagine it any other way.'

Above: Alexandra's blue pigment has become a signature in her work.
Opposite: Alexandra's vessels are functional but have a strong sculptural feel.

Alison Fraser

Alison Fraser didn't pursue art or ceramics school or college, and she spent much of her adult career as a graphic designer and copywriter in her own agency. With the arrival of her first child, she sold the agency. After her second child was born, Alison turned her thoughts to making handmade tiles.

Something about this new phase of motherhood drew on Alison's own childhood. Her very first exposure to hands-on ceramics was seeing her mother make pottery in the 1970s, at a time when handicrafts were enjoying a revival. 'Her pottery class was based in some old cow-shed in a nearby field, and I loved hanging out there with Mum and the other women. I have a vivid memory of slanted light coming through the old slats, catching white dust in the air from the dry clay while I fossicked for discarded shards of pottery treasure. As I fiddled around in the dirt, I listened to the soft contented chat of the women as they wedged the clay and made their pots,' Alison remembers. 'Mum had a good instinctive aesthetic, simple forms in heavily grogged clay, and only partially glazed to expose the natural clay body. Her choices then are imprinted on my work today.'

As time passed, Alison shifted her focus away from ceramic tiles. She found that she was increasingly distracted by flatware and other functional pieces,

and has now been making these pieces for four years, working with heavily grogged stoneware clay. 'As I have no formal technical training I have taught myself through reading, research and trial and error. The coarser the clay, the more forgiving it is, which helps a klutz like me,' she says.

Aside from the early inspiration gained from her mother, guidance has come from many sources. A trip to Japan a couple of years ago revealed to Alison that leaving things loose and unstructured is not only acceptable but is, at times, a treasured aesthetic – a sentiment that she found liberating. She also later attended workshops by renowned ceramicist Kwi Rak Choung, who asked her what she most enjoyed doing. 'My answer was getting my hands stuck into the clay, so his advice was to stick to hand building and not worry about the wheel. It was the best advice ever,' says Alison.

Being a hand builder, Alison's practice is repetitive and meditative. She is soothed by the calmness that comes with repetitive motions, the tactile nature of practice and the sound of hands smacking the clay. She began making functional pieces as gifts, finding satisfaction in making something to give to people she cherishes. 'It represents time I have devoted to them. Selling work is just icing on the cake.'

Left: Alison relaxing on the porch at home.

Alison also enjoys the technical challenges of clay that engage her intellectually. She usually approaches problem-solving, and the research necessary to resolve issues around firing, for example, on her own. 'Just the learning process and overcoming technical problems is satisfying. I am thankful now for a traditional education that included chemistry, physics and biology, as all sciences come into play in ceramics.'

Unlike many of her contemporaries, who delight in a freshly opened kiln and a full load of successful firings, Alison often doesn't initially like her pieces. 'It can take a while for me to see the merits of a piece. About six months ago I started a series of bottle forms but stopped, partly distracted by another project, but also because I was quite dissatisfied by the bottles. They sat on the workbench for months. I recently revisited them and decided that I didn't mind them. I subsequently showed the bottles to someone whose opinion I very much respect – who declared them beautiful,' she recalls. 'I had a distinct flush of pride and pleasure in that moment.

Alison feels the current desire for handcrafted work is driven by a response not only to mass production, but also to a growing global population of over seven billion. 'That makes people feel anonymous and unimportant,' she says. 'It is a *cri de cœur* for individuality and uniqueness that drives both the increase in the practice and the desire to have one-off pieces in the home.'

Above and opposite: Alison's bottle forms are not glazed; instead a cobalt stain is applied to the surface after bisque firing. Unlike traditional use of cobalt, Alison prefers the blue to be dominant, where normally white would major.

CLAY

Above and opposite: Alison's pieces are hand built, which gives them a loose, unstructured aesthetic.

Andrei Davidoff

For Andrei Davidoff, knowing that someone could be handling one of his ceramics every day gives him a heightened mindfulness in his work. He feels this sense of responsibility because it means that he's potentially having an impact on part of a person's day-to-day routine.

Andrei first encountered ceramics when staying with a friend who is a wood-fire potter in rural New South Wales. He spent several months helping his friend around the studio. 'That was the introduction I had to the discipline, and where I gained a respect for the materials that carried through my subsequent studies,' he explains. A few years later, Andrei moved to Melbourne and began a Bachelor of Fine Arts at RMIT, majoring in ceramics, followed by a Master of Fine Arts, which he completed in 2012.

Now a full-time practising ceramicist, Andrei works in several streams, including functional production ware, studio pottery and conceptual work. He describes the overarching elements of these as simple, classical forms, with minimal glazes and a tendency towards block colour – particularly black.

Andrei makes his production ware with reduction-fired porcelain and stoneware clays, often blending and making his clay bodies and developing his own glazes. These pieces are predominantly wheel thrown and altered with some hand building. His conceptual and exhibition work uses earthenware, stoneware and everything in between, both fired and unfired, using commercial glazes and his own.

What he loves is the responsiveness of clay as a medium, and the large and ever-present element of unpredictability, which he describes as both a blessing and a curse. Andrei also acknowledges that failure is an integral part of the ceramic process. 'Once you get over the problems enshrined in making ceramics, any other hurdle – be it design- or concept-wise – is almost insignificant,' he says.

Andrei is also economical in praising his own successes. 'Regardless of how proud you may feel after any exhibition, grant and residency – clay will bring you back down to earth quick smart.' When asked for his best advice to up-and-comers, he responds, 'Technique will give you freedom.'

Naming renowned potters Lisa Hammond and Edmund de Waal as his constant ceramic muses, Andrei also notes that that he is undeniably influenced by the Anglo–Oriental ceramic tradition, taking into account both its positives and negatives. 'Clay has a long and fascinating history which can be constantly examined, reinterpreted and subverted,' he explains.

Left: Andrei at work in
his studio.

'You'd think that after so
many failures and misfires
your heart would become
a bit more guarded; yet every
dunted plate, cracked handle
and fractured sculpture is still
a little cardiac moment.'

Above: Andrei's *Function Verge* series is made from wheel-thrown stoneware clay, which he makes himself. The thrown pieces are cut and assembled with hand-built additions, then semi-glazed. Opposite: The *Brushwork* production series work is wheel-thrown, reduction-fired, unglazed polished porcelain with black slip used for decoration.

Anna-Karina

Anna-Karina came to ceramics through a simple desire to make herself a bowl. In the beginning, she could only commit to one day of clay work per week, but that soon changed as ceramics consumed her. 'Something clicked, and I now live and breathe it. I've been doing it every day for seven years,' she says.

Anna-Karina's pieces are simple and pared back, with a natural, organic quality to them. After a busy previous life in fashion and interiors, it was a move from Sydney to Byron Bay that signalled a change of pace and also of creative focus. 'I live in the country by the sea, and I studied biodynamic agriculture for a while. I feel the lessons of observing nature and its forms give us clues to the natural rhythms of life, and these are often reflected in my work,' she explains.

Ceramics, for Anna-Karina, represent a way of telling her story. It includes visits to an ancient past, rituals, artefactual forms and an undeniably tactile engagement. 'I can express all my emotions and ideas in my work. I can struggle internally with a concept and process it through my work. If someone understands my language that's a bonus, if not and they take it at face value, that's OK too,' she says.

Anna-Karina loves the intimacy to working with clay, and the fact that it demands a physical and mental interaction. Professing to be naturally introspective and highly sensitive, she is consumed not just by how the work will look, but also by how it feels, and how it will evoke a certain response. 'There is no distant objectivity for either the viewer or myself,' she explains. 'I find it hard to articulate what I want to say or how I feel ... My art, I feel, communicates for me. As the maker, my breath and spirit are worked into the clay itself, all the examination of my consciousness and observations are unconsciously imbued into the individual pieces.'

Although she started out very traditionally and focused on throwing, over time Anna-Karina has learned a variety of methods through studying with different teachers. She now uses a mix of techniques. Hand building, mould making, and throwing on both electric and kick wheels are all incorporated into her practice, and she will choose the technique and material best suited to the piece she is making – whether it be stoneware, porcelain or earthenware.

As with any art practice, once you start investigating your medium, questions start to arise. 'You start exploring and examining who you are. For the longest time I struggled with the legitimacy of my work. I was reluctant to put myself out in the public

Left: Anna-Karina at work in her studio.

eye and I wrestled with the economic exchange, with ideas about value and art-versus-commercialism. These thoughts started to be corrosive. It took me quite a while before I mentally committed myself to a life of creating,' she acknowledges. 'I'm most proud of the fact I know irrefutably that I want to create and that the work I do is a transformative journey'.

Such certainty does not remove the practical challenges of a ceramics career. 'Cost is a major issue. It's expensive to set up and run your equipment, and to buy your ingredients. I work alone and I have difficulty trying to balance the business side of things,' she says.

Anna-Karina also describes a kind of snobbery when it comes to making utilitarian work. 'Many people want to validate ceramic art, and verbalizing your approach can sometimes reduce it to a linear perspective,' she explains. 'Describing work is not always relevant, especially when the work is made for a visual and physical experience.'

To those just starting out in ceramics, Anna-Karina's advice is sage. 'Find your own voice; don't look at social media to see what other people are doing. Be authentically you. Don't give up. It's not easy and it can be all too frustrating at times. Importantly, never stop the technical practice. I often see students with clumsy work; wabi-sabi is not permission to make poor-quality work.'

Above: Anna-Karina's piece is quadruple fired with four different layers of glaze.
Opposite: Two mixed-stoneware plates with a matte-white calcium glaze. The calcium comes from shells collected on the beach near Anna-Karina's home.

'One has to engage with the pieces, see them, touch them, experience them. The work becomes a multi-sensorial experience.'

Anna Lerinder

Above: Anna enjoys the challenges inherent in her work.

Anna Lerinder was educated as a designer at Beckmans College of Design in Stockholm. 'My plan wasn't to work with ceramics. My plan was to work in different materials, but my first job after school was at Rörstrand – a well-known Swedish porcelain brand – and so I went on!' she says. 'I worked at Rörstrand for one year, then I left to start my freelance life in my own studio in 1998. To get assignments I started to do my own designs … and the rest is history. Ceramics is my life. I'm interested in timeless beauty and, for me, that is what clay represents.'

Significant to Anna's work are strong form and proportion, and she is interested in light, shadow, movement and surface. 'These are the tools in my environment that I use to inspire how I approach a special task, and it's the same process for both small pieces and big wall work. I have always worked with clay and I have always been interested in form. I have really early memories of thinking about form even if it wasn't formulated as it is today,' she explains.

'I cast and I build, and I use bone china and stoneware. What I enjoy about this medium is that you can use the same material in so many different ways and get so many expressions,' says Anna. Because of its level of difficulty, Anna has always found delicate bone china interesting to work with, and she embraces the challenge it presents. 'When you do master it, you have a lovely product in your hands that is both delicate and strong. For opposite reasons, it's nice to work with stoneware, as it has a completely different character. I like to colour the stoneware in black, as it's a nice contrast to the bone china,' she says. 'I think the bone china stands for light and the stoneware for darkness and density. And I need both.'

Anna uses forms to cast her work. Because she originally believed that she would only ever work in the mainstream ceramics industry, she trained as a modeller. 'But the porcelain industry died in Sweden, and I felt that I'd better do things by myself,' she explains.

Anna says that she is very influenced by the designers working in the art industry in the early and mid-1900s – including glass, ceramics and porcelain, as well as the established Swedish design

houses of Rörstrand, Gustavsberg and Orrefors. 'The designers, for example at Gustavsberg, worked with everyday ware such as cups and plates, but also with great wall decorations in public spaces. I really like the dynamics in the differences between small and big work. When it comes to style I try to be true to myself, but I have always been interested in Japanese craft and design. I love their way of working with proportions.'

The satisfaction that Anna derives from her practice comes from working with new ideas and seeing things come to life. 'It is also always to good hear from people that they love your work,' she says. 'To be successful you have to possess patience, and to a degree be very strong-headed. It is also important to love your own work.'

Above: Anna enjoys the play of light and shadow across the surface of her pieces.

'Clay represents
timelessness. It's
old and modern,
and if you don't
break it, it will
last for hundreds,
maybe thousands
of years.'

Above: Anna's hand-painted bone china bowls.
Opposite: Large white and grey bottles, made from glazed
moulded stoneware and coloured stoneware cast.
Following pages: Form and proportion are important
aspects of Anna's work.

CLAY

Ashraf Hanna

Ashraf Hanna has always been driven by the need to explore and strive for excellence. He celebrates making as the product of observation and thought, and the physical manifestation of ideas and skills. His first interaction with pottery forms within a creative environment occurred while Ashraf was closely observing ceramics during drawing classes at the Faculty of Fine Arts at Minia University in Egypt. He became aware of the quiet beauty and sense of contentment that exist within a considered and sensitively executed form. The many hours spent drawing improved his mark-making skills and, more importantly, allowed time for contemplation and subsequent liberation from prejudices and old perceptions regarding functional pottery.

Ashraf originally trained as a set and costume designer at Central Saint Martins College of Art and Design in London, and it was not until his early thirties, when he met his future wife, the sculptor Sue Hanna, that he discovered 'making' with clay. Sue taught him how to make his first hand-built pot and Ashraf was immediately hooked. 'For our first holiday we responded to an ad in *Ceramic Review* promising sunshine and pit-fired pots in an unspoilt hilly Greek village working with Scottish potter Alan Bain. It sounded wonderful and it was! I came back from the holiday in love with both the woman and the pots. I found true joy in making, which set me on a career path that continues to this day,' Ashraf recalls.

Between 1999 and 2009 Ashraf's career was largely concerned with exploring raku and smoke-fired work, with no formal training. 'In 2009 I decided to take time out from a successful and hectic exhibition schedule to embark on a two-year MA at the Royal College of Art in London, allowing time and space for new ideas to be born,' he says.

Ashraf makes hand-built forms, creating groups and individual vessels, with each object informing the next. The profiles, lines and spaces emerging from this process of development, their ultimate placement in relation to one another, and the juxtaposition of sharp lines and softer curves, have become his major interest and serve to emphasize the sculptural aspects in his work. 'My current work is minimalist, focusing on form. The pared-down surfaces invite the eye to engage with developing lines with no interference from heavily decorated surfaces,' he explains.

Starting each piece as a pinch pot, Ashraf then develops the form using soft slabs. When leather-hard, the form is refined using metal kidneys. After

Left: Ashraf at work on one of his sculptural vessels.

the biscuit firing, the piece is further refined, then the final surface treatment is applied. Layers of fine lips (coloured terra sigillata) are sprayed on to create depth and to highlight the subtle surface texture.

Ashraf reflects on an occasion in April 2014 that left a creative mark on him. 'I attended a London Symphony Orchestra concert of the music of Estonian-born composer Arvo Pärt and Tunisian-born musician Dhafer Youssef. Both had such a profound effect on me, and I intend to immerse myself in their music as I work in my new studio!' he enthuses.

Continually inspired by multitudes, Ashraf feels that we are the product of what surrounds us — whether it is architecture, the human figure, sand dunes, various landscapes or, indeed, music — and our life experiences shape our vision of the world and what we ultimately value as beautiful or important.

As to the joys and challenges of clay, Ashraf remains philosophical. 'It does not matter how many years of experience one has, it is always about the next firing. Equally it does not matter how many beautiful pots one has made in the past, it is always about the next pot.'

CLAY

'Whilst the utilitarian nature of a piece might determine the shape and surface treatments, the form itself has physical presence, also worthy of study.'

Above and opposite: The groupings of Ashraf's work create interesting juxtapositions, with each piece in dialogue with the next.

Brigitte Colleaux

Brigitte Colleaux makes tableware decorated exclusively with wood-ash glazes, keeping her forms simple to give the glazes a 'voice'. 'I feel like I am an alchemist when I play with ashes in my glazes,' she says. Her influences are many, ranging from snowy landscapes to the nuka ash glazes of Karatsu, kohiki and white hagi ware.

Working with clay sourced from Cornwall, Brigitte fires her work in an electric kiln, which produces an oxidizing atmosphere. This is perhaps surprising given her dedication to ash glazes, which actually work best in a reduction atmosphere. She does admit that she finds it more difficult to get interesting results. 'It requires lots of testing with raw materials, but this in itself is exciting. If I could reduction-fire, I would pay more attention to what clay bodies I use and place the pots in strategic spots in the kiln to get interesting effects,' she says. On the matter of kilns, Brigitte dispenses some guidance to burgeoning potters. 'Get a bigger kiln than you think you need, if you can afford it. As you get better and quicker at making, a small kiln just becomes uneconomical and frustrating!'

Brigitte's adventurous spirit with clay belies a previous career in IT, working full-time for a bank. Feeling that something was lacking, she longed for a more creative pursuit. During the late 1990s, she took painting and drawing lessons at her local arts centre, which also offered textiles, photography and pottery courses. 'On a whim, I decided to enrol in the pottery class, and I have never looked back,' she explains.

Initially Brigitte was only practising her pottery once a week, but she soon found herself taking exams and getting hooked. Her teacher was a professional potter who lived off his craft, and he introduced Brigitte to a world of which she had previously been unaware. 'Seeing my enthusiasm, his advice was that I should visit other professional potters to gain more experience,' she says. 'I didn't go to university or complete an apprenticeship. Instead, I have invested a lot of time in watching other potters throw and fire their kilns, taking courses here and there.'

Brigitte often visits the British and Victoria and Albert Museums for inspiration. She is grateful to all the unknown potters who have produced the beautiful celadon works that she so admires, as well as the Thai potters who made the fish-decorated bowls that were rescued from the sea after being shipwrecked in Southeast Asia. She also has several contemporary ceramics muses, among them British potters who were once her teachers.

Brigitte is encouraged by the current interest in rediscovering locally made, handcrafted objects. 'People want to make choices for themselves and when an object has a provenance and a story to tell, I think it has more meaning. I think this applies to other crafts as well, such as sewing, cooking and bread-making,' says Brigitte. 'In the case of ceramics, it will hopefully give a renewed interest in the craft of the potter and put a stop to the closure of pottery courses in the UK and elsewhere.'

'Glazes are the most
exciting aspect of my work.
I test for the sake of it, often
with no objective in mind!
There are no borders –
you become an explorer,
and an adventurer.'

Above: Brigitte's tableware is decorated exclusively with wood-ash glazes, which
work to emphasize the surface texture of the pieces.

Above: Brigitte works with clay sourced from Cornwall.
Opposite: Brigitte is inspired by experimentation during the glazing process, and loves the challenge of its inherent alchemy.

Cécile Daladier

Cécile Daladier's career is dedicated to visual arts, and ceramics is but one medium among others in her practice, which includes painting, wax, metal and plants. Over the last five years Cécile decided to focus on ceramics, simply because it fascinated her. Cécile lives and practises in the Drôme district in southern France, an area where ceramics is traditionally an important craft.

Most recently, Cécile has been creating a significant range of ceramic vessels designed for arranging twigs, leaves and flowers. While she is influenced by older pieces of traditional ceramics as well as by modern art and design, it is ultimately the flower that Cécile has in mind that informs the vase. Often those flowers give their names to her vases, such as the *Tulipier* and the *Violettier*. Another influencing aspect is the water. Cécile makes unconventionally shaped pieces that leave the surface of the water visible. 'I've also created what I call table gardens, which are shallow, wide vases with different types of holes in order to put all kinds of flowers and recreate a small garden,' Cécile explains.

Cécile's vases are all unique, each carrying its own personality. Some have holes or slits and they can be deep or shallow, narrow or wide. Others have pipes and chimneys to create a sort of sculpture. 'What is important to keep in mind is that you don't want the flowers to be packed or crowded. They need to breathe and the holes allow that,' she explains. 'The flowers that I put in my vases are all flowers that also shape my vases. I really want to stay away from the traditional round bouquet that you buy in a shop and stick in your vase as it is.'

Cécile sees clay as a temporal and universal medium and, in her work, clay and plants are almost inseparable. Her vessels are hand formed and wood fired in her homemade kiln. They are then smoked with materials gathered around her studio, such as wild plants, clay, enamel, fallen leaves and dry grass. Cécile is especially fond of the fact that the processes of firing and glazing are full of unpredictable elements and you can never be certain of the outcome. She likes that clay is directly shaped by the hand, allowing a chance for spontaneity and improvization.

Cécile expresses a preference for the momentary, the ephemeral and the small in life. 'I hate spectacular. What interests me are the daily-life things. I love banal, common flowers. I get inspiration from my surroundings and I hope that's what comes out in my vases: simple and uncomplicated. My approach is very intuitive. My style relies mostly on the contemplation of nature. It emphasizes the oppositions between the fleeting and the permanent, botanical and mineral, movement and stillness.'

Previous page: The flowers surrounding Cécile's studio inform the shapes
of her vases.
Above and opposite: Cécile's *Table Garden* vessels are designed for arranging
individual twigs, leaves and flowers – quite unlike traditional florist-bought
bouquets. The form of the vessel allows the flowers to 'breathe'.

'There is no real distinction
between beauty and use.
If it's useful, it's beautiful,
and vice versa.'

Above: The pipes and chimneys in Cécile's vessels give them a sculptural feel.
Opposite: Cécile's studio in the Drôme district of southern France.

Claire Johnson

Above: Claire uses hand-building techniques for most of her pieces.

When Claire Johnson was at school, her art class was directed to recreate the grand sculptures of artist Henry Moore using clay. 'I think it was love at that very moment. Through all the mess and the clumsy way my hands gripped the medium at first, it soon turned into a fascination, and so began my greatest passion,' she says. She later completed a Bachelor of Fine Arts at the University of New South Wales Art & Design, majoring in ceramics.

Claire is predominantly a hand builder, rolling slabs to either even or uneven thickness held together with liquid slip. 'So far white grog raku is my favourite clay, as I find that the grog is best for me when I'm building. It helps me to build larger objects as well as creating an amazing texture,' she explains. 'One of the things I love most about ceramics is the way it seems to respond so naturally to touch. How just one movement, mark or impression can completely change something you're working on.'

Claire believes that taking time out to paint every now and again really helps her to resolve her next sculpture, or to create an image that she wishes to transfer to ceramics. 'Painting and ceramics go hand in hand for me in my practice, each influencing the other,' she says. 'As an artist your work is constantly evolving. The one thing that doesn't really change all that much for me is my "painterly" approach.' Claire acknowledges that it is difficult to pinpoint her exact influences and inspirations, as there have been so many. 'If I had to mention one though, it's probably Australian artist Rhys Lee. I'll never forget the day I saw his exhibition *Long Knives* at Sydney's Arthouse Gallery. The way his ceramics and paintings spoke to each other has stayed with me, and I can identify with that,' she says.

Working in ceramics means that challenges come in many different forms, but Claire accepts them all. 'Whether it's an unsuccessful glaze firing, a sculpture I've been working on for weeks meeting a horrible fate or just generally living that broke artist life. Sometimes it's hard but I really can't see myself doing anything else. Just like any relationship, you take the good with the bad when you're really in love with something.'

Above: Claire's works often feature bright colours and images.

Deciding to get a studio just two weeks after graduation stands as one of Claire's best decisions to date. 'I don't think it's hard to justify paying for a space to work in when that space really becomes your sanctuary, which is what my studio is for me. I would encourage any student upon leaving university or college to invest in a studio space. Having a separate place to work away from home brings so much more productivity and fresh thought. Working from my shared studio I am constantly surrounded by other creatives who, in their own way, inspire me daily. It also works as your own support network – it's nice having people around you who also work in the creative field to share in successes, failures and the occasional rant! I also think it's wonderful that people are taking an interest in a medium I love and work with. If the clay trend ever cools though I'll still be here, elbow-deep in the stuff. I'm in this for life!'

Above and opposite: Painting and ceramics both have an important place in Claire's creative practice.

'I guess I've always loved all the imperfections in my work, thumbprints especially! I'm really passionate about the idea of the "artist's hand".'

Dawn Vachon

One wouldn't think that an early career as a baker would necessarily lead to ceramics, but that was precisely the case for Canadian-born Dawn Vachon. As a baker Dawn loved the malleability of her medium and working with her hands, but she found the fleeting nature of baked goods left her wishing for a creative outlet with more permanence.

Enrolling in art school in 2004, she tried a bit of everything, each year narrowing in on preferences, but Dawn knew by the end of the first year that she would be focusing on ceramics. Her studies in Vancouver spanned four years, covering skills, cultural theory and art history, and later material that was more conceptual and design-oriented.

Naming Ron Nagle – an American sculptor, musician and songwriter known for his very detailed and colourful small-scale sculptures – as her ceramics muse, Dawn describes her own style as 'inconsistent and ever-changing'. As her slab range was in demand for a time, Dawn spent many tedious hours making these fussy pieces. Eventually, and in response to that experience, she began to loosen up and started simultaneously creating simple forms with very free and moody surface treatments, as well as some lumpy, chunky, oddly colourful and fun pieces. These pieces employed a mix of wheel throwing and hand building, stoneware, mid-fire clays and glazes, white clay with speckle and often stain colourants added directly to the clay. And in that versatility is the beauty of her work.

Discussion of clay as a material nearly always elicits some deliciously visceral and emotive responses from ceramic artists – and for Dawn she admits one of the joys of her practice is the smell of clay itself. She also confesses an addiction to the suspense and surprise of seeing what comes out of the kiln.

Interestingly, it is the challenge of Dawn's practice and the constraints within which she works that most influence her work, and to that end they are welcomed. 'I find I need restrictions to work within, otherwise there are too many possibilities and I feel overwhelmed. The main restrictions that I have at the moment are a small studio and how I transport my work, unfired, in a trailer that I tow with my bicycle to the kiln service. So my forms are usually simple and sturdy so they can withstand the jostle. Likewise, I began colouring my clay many years ago as a way of achieving colour and pattern when the complex glaze work that I was previously using was often ruined in transport,' explains Dawn.

Dawn has concerns about the current appetite for ceramics, primarily with the mass of poorly crafted work that is being made and sold freely. 'I hope that anyone who has bought a crappy slab cheese board that broke on the first use hasn't written off the quality and durability of all handmade ceramics straight away!' she says.

Left: Dawn colours her clay rather than using complex glazes.

'I like blocked colour and simple patterns – things that look really simple but are actually quite complicated.'

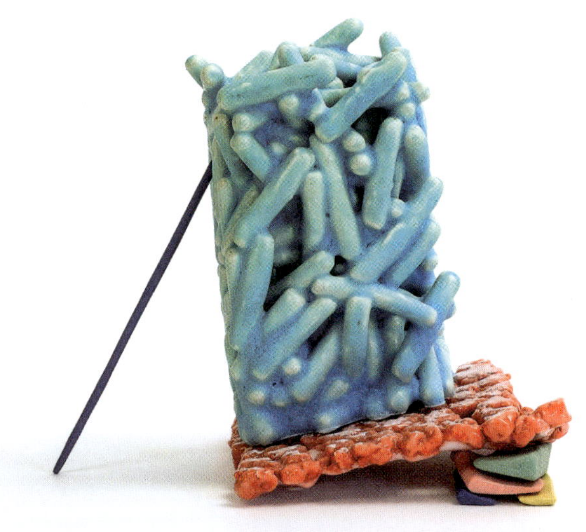

Above: Dawn uses multiple clays, mid-fired glazes, and stained feldspar in her sculptural pieces, which are rendered in her signature block colours.
Opposite: Dawn sketching in her studio.

LITIUM CARB
BONE ASH SYNTHETIC
ALUMINA HYDRATE
STRONTIUM CARB
MANGANESE CARB
MANGANESE DIOX
SODA ASH
ZINC OXIDE
ZIRCOSIL
TIN OX
TITANIUM DIOXIDE
ICE ICE BABY

Derek Wilson

The historical context of ceramics has always been pertinent to Derek Wilson's practice. His view is that clay ware is ubiquitous – from tiles to bricks and everyday utilitarian pieces. The way people collect and treasure ceramic objects – whether they are purely decorative, sentimental or just for function – has always fascinated him. 'It is a discipline that I am proud of and I value its diverse history.'

Derek particularly enjoys the fluidity and repetition of production, as well as finding the subtle nuances and variations when working on functional pieces. There is a freedom in experimenting and discovering new processes, materials or finishes that motivates his practice, and the translation of ideas or sketches into three-dimensional forms is one of his greatest thrills. Overcoming technical restraints and the challenges that clay consistently throws at the maker, and having the skills to quickly and efficiently produce creative solutions, bring a satisfaction that comes only from mastering your craft.

Derek was initially introduced to clay during his foundation studies at Bournemouth and Poole College of Art. He was drawn to the experimental nature and the endless possibilities of clay as a material, and this led him to study ceramics for his degree. Derek recalls that this period of his work was predominantly sculptural, as he had very little interest in functional ceramics or using the potter's wheel. After his degree he became more focused on the idea of learning a skill, which led him to apply for a traditional throwing-skills course run by the Design & Crafts Council of Ireland. It proved to be a very intense and challenging course, but immensely rewarding. The skills enabled Derek to execute his own work, and also to gain an understanding of the importance of handmade qualities inherent in wheel-thrown objects. 'The course gave me the skills to work as an apprentice potter for some production potteries in Ireland. These potteries were mainly tourist-orientated, an area that I did not especially appreciate, yet I wanted to focus and develop my production skills before setting up my own studio.'

Derek initially struggled to find a studio space and found the task of starting up both expensive and daunting, which led him back to studying for his masters at Ulster University in Northern Ireland. He returned to sculptural work and now predominantly uses the potter's wheel. 'Upon completing my MA I decided to set up a practice concentrating on porcelain tableware, with the initial idea being to balance the production of sculptural objects with a small run of functional pieces, therefore enabling me to sustain my overall practice,' Derek explains.

Simplicity of form has always been the overriding quality and aesthetic within Derek's practice. He is ever aware of the quality of an object and the skill it takes to produce. Porcelain is the prevalent material used for his tableware pieces, and more recently he has introduced other clay bodies such as terracotta, as well as mixing up his own coloured clay. For his

Left: Derek strives for simplicity of form in his tableware.

sculptural objects Derek uses a slightly grogged stoneware, with the forms made in sections, given the slightly more forgiving nature of this material when compared to porcelain. The majority of his work is still thrown on the potter's wheel, with the exception of some sculptural pieces, which are hand built from slabs of rolled out clay. 'I have always had a very minimal and reductive approach towards the execution of my work. I tend to simplify the form and surface, taking away and reducing any source of distraction. Much more recently I have been experimenting with some sgraffito detail on the tableware, yet it still holds a minimalistic approach,' he says.

Derek has long been inspired by art movements such as Russian and British Constructivism, De Stijl, Minimalism, and Bauhaus, as well as the work produced during the Festival of Britain. 'I tend to be greatly influenced by and drawn to painters such as Ben Nicholson and William Scott, both artists who had a tendency to focus on the abstraction of everyday utilitarian objects,' says Derek.

'My environment is also important,' he says. 'The industrial heritage within Belfast where I am based can absorb and work its way into my work. Ideas can also evolve and develop out of processes and experimentation with the materials and techniques I am using when pieces are successful and new ideas or forms appear. I am always amazed at how much more there is to learn within this discipline and I guess that is something that keeps me interested in working within the field of ceramics.'

Above and opposite: Porcelain is the prevalent material used for Derek's tableware pieces, but he has recently introduced other clay bodies, such as terracotta, as well as mixing up his own coloured clay.

'I tend to focus on the interaction between objects, which is why I show my work in selected groupings. The interaction and the relevance of the space in between is what interests me.'

Florian Gadsby

Florian Gadsby's high school had a very well-equipped pottery department and a brilliant throwing tutor – and yet, surprisingly, he was the only student who took ceramics as a subject. Having observed his teacher throw with what seemed like such ease and control, Florian was immediately hooked, spending all of his time between classes and after school at the pottery wheel with the aim of one day having the same ability. Despite this, it was not a vocational path he really expected to pursue.

Florian loved working with his hands more than anything, and was always intrigued by three-dimensional arts and crafts, practising both metalwork and woodwork before he recognized his true passion was ceramics. He completed the two-year Ceramic Skills and Design Course at the Design & Crafts Council of Ireland, which trained him not only to throw at a production level, but also to develop an individual style and character within his ceramics, which Florian says gave him a 'voice and fluency' in clay.

Successful in obtaining a sought-after two-year apprenticeship at the well-known Maze Hill Pottery studio and school in London in 2014, Florian currently works with renowned soda-firing potter, Lisa Hammond, while maintaining his own practice on the side, focusing mainly on functional ceramics thrown on the wheel.

When working for Lisa, Florian does everything that goes with running a normal studio: mixing clay and glazes, cleaning and keeping the place organized, wrapping pots for delivery, throwing the standard ware range for Maze Hill Pottery, packing the student kiln and helping Lisa pack and fire the soda kilns. When he does have free days, Florian spends them almost entirely working on his own pots.

There is certainly a calmness and tranquility to Florian's work which, despite his short tenure, has earned him many admirers. His functional pieces, inspired by the simple, un-fussy aesthetic of Japanese household pottery, are finished in whites, blues, greens, greys and blacks which belie the complexity of his glazes and allow the simplicity of form to speak. The earthy, geological colours that he prefers relate back to where the materials come from. The methods by which mud and stone are turned into permanent, delicate objects from the ground is a wonder not lost on Florian. 'Knowing that what I've made may last for eternity is quite special,' he says.

Craftsmanship is another principle aspect of Florian's practice, with the overall finish of his pieces

Left: Florian throwing one pound breakfast bowls using a clay high in iron.

being paramount. He describes one of the challenges of making ceramics as developing and creating a library of work that he is content with, and also one that he is satisfied with existing out there in the world to be used and scrutinized by people. 'More than anything I don't want to fall into the trap of making work that sells but that I don't particularly like. In a market that's so interested in how cheaply something can be manufactured and mass produced, attempting to sell my work for what it's honestly worth can be difficult, and that makes the market hard to enter and be successful in,' he explains.

Despite the challenges of commerciality, Florian is rooted in the idea that pottery is one of the oldest crafts of the human race and is central to how humanity developed. 'The methods have barely

changed in thousands of years. Losing such an important craft as we enter a digital age would be devastating, as it represents centuries of historical advancement, culture and beauty,' says Florian.

For a young ceramicist who has achieved so much in a relatively short time, Florian's proudest achievement is a humble one. 'It's likely when somebody tells me that they use one of my pots every day, that it's their go-to bowl for breakfast or it's their favourite mug,' says Florian. 'I'm proud to be able to make objects that have such importance in people's lives, even if they're just little moments like that. It's what encourages me to keep making.'

CLAY

'Function has always influenced me more than sculptural or highly decorative work. I'm interested in making pieces that have an individual use, such as ceramic pens, inkwells and watercolour palettes.'

Above: Florian's functional pieces are inspired by the aesthetic of Japanese household pottery.
Opposite: His glazes are all in earthy shades which belie their complexity, allowing for the simplicity of form to speak.

Frances Palmer

Frances Palmer has been prolific in pottery for almost thirty years, and it's fair to say there is a certain amount of the urban legend about her work. She holds an undergraduate and graduate degree in art history, so was long familiar with ceramics and civilization. However, it took a permanent move from New York to Connecticut to raise her young family to prompt her to make pots for herself. This work unifies her garden, her cooking and her love of making with her hands, with all of these interests richly informing her craft. 'Because I love to grow flowers in the garden, and I love to bake and I love to display things, these passions inspire the forms and functions of my pieces.'

There is both wit and whimsy in Frances' pottery, with its purposeful imperfections and the undeniable functionality of her pieces. It is evident at first glance that her vases are made to hold flowers and her cake plates to serve baked goods. The goal she sets for her work is to be both functional and artful. 'I don't make or grow things to hold onto them, but rather to send them out into the world for others to live with and enjoy. My handmade ceramics are functional art – dishware or vases that can be used on a daily basis. Each piece, no matter how large or small, is considered and individual.'

Frances enjoys the hand-throwing process, and it can take anywhere from four days to two weeks to make each of her pieces. She works mostly on the wheel, preferring white earthenware, terracotta and high-fire translucent porcelain. She likes to throw forms in sections and then put them together for drama, often including a bit of hand building to augment the forms. In the white earthenware, her footed vases with detailing such as beads and fluting are signatures. In porcelain, she keeps the forms graceful and focuses on classic Chinese and Japanese glazes, such as celadon, oxblood and shino.

Regardless of her experience, Frances feels making pots is an ongoing journey where one needs enormous patience and perseverance. 'You have to be prepared for failure and yet still enjoy the process,' she reflects. 'There are many aspects to making pots that are out of one's control and I find it all a metaphor for many things in life.'

Often, making one piece will lead Frances in a new direction. Things that she might initially deem a mistake turn out to be a different road and new inspiration that she begins to follow. She also gathers inspiration by looking and reading widely. 'I see as many exhibitions as possible, not necessarily ceramic,

Left: Frances's works often include intricate details such as beads and fluting.

and read constantly. I subscribe to many design blogs and try to keep up with what is happening in the ceramics world as well as in food, design, gardening and fashion,' she says. 'I am always excited to sit at the wheel to throw and explore form. Ceramics has connected societies for thousands of years. I spend a good deal of time studying pots from different centuries and relating them to my ideas. That being said – it takes discipline to have one's own business, and I am inclined to work every day. Sometimes, I have to make myself step away and take a rest.'

Although her aesthetic has remained fairly constant since she began making ceramics, Frances continually works on her craft and her technical skills, feeling that there is still much to learn. 'The best piece of life advice that I received was that if you begin something, you should follow it through to the

end. That may sound simple, however, sometimes one has to push to get through a situation and not quit midway,' she shares. 'The best business advice that I received was not to look left or right, but straight ahead. Meaning, you cannot worry about what your competitors are doing. You must believe in and keep to your vision, as that is what will move you along.'

Above and opposite: Celadon vases holding Frances' homegrown blooms.

'I love the texture of the clay.
I love the feeling of it rising
up into a shape that I thought
of in my brain, and yet at the
same time I let it go and see
what it does for itself.'

Georgia Harvey

Despite a background in the arts studying painting and art conservation, Georgia Harvey struggled initially to maintain an ongoing art practice, feeling that she never had the drive to make a proper go of it. A few years ago, while working as a conservator at the National Gallery of Victoria, she rather abruptly developed an interest in ceramics. The small spark of latent creativity that she'd been hoarding for years was suddenly and quite dramatically ignited.

Georgia's interest in ceramics coincided with a time when her young children were starting to gain some independence, and she felt she could begin to reclaim a bit of her pre-parenthood identity. Largely self-taught (though frequently calling on the advice of a generous and well-connected international clay community, and participating in workshops), Georgia spent a year or so exploring techniques and materials, before starting to exhibit and sell her work full-time in 2013.

Claiming not to have been working long enough to find her specific ceramics 'style', Georgia describes her work as possessing a painterly quality. She has a fondness for burnished, rounded forms that invite touch, but equally enjoys garish colour, unrefined surfaces and lumpy glazes. 'I am fascinated with material interaction and failure. Relinquishing some control to the vagaries of the fire is a very appealing part of the process,' she explains.

As a painter, Georgia would build up and then 'excavate' surfaces to allow imagery to emerge. It is possible that this has informed her approach to ceramics, with a similar process detached from specific intention. 'I enjoy surprises,' she says.

Georgia endeavours to render her practice as close to carbon-neutral as she can, reclaiming and reusing all her scrap materials, including glaze slops, as well as collecting old materials from garage sales. While she admits that at times this predetermines what she is able to make, she enjoys working within some limitations, stating that it ultimately encourages creative thinking.

Firing at her home in small electric kilns, Georgia has gone so far as to install solar power to offset the energy they use. 'This is particularly important to me as I often glaze-fire pieces more than once to get the surfaces I like,' she explains. Tending to stay at the low temperature end of the ceramics spectrum minimizes energy consumption and allows for the effects she wants to achieve. 'My earliest firings were raku and although I have experimented with a range of

Left: Georgia raku fires her work at relatively low temperatures. In order to create a crackle effect in the glaze, she places still-hot pieces into a closed container filled with combustible materials.

techniques from one end of the pyrometric chart to the other, I love the speed and drama of raku. I also love the transformative power of reduction, and thermal shock,' says Georgia.

Not surprisingly, the collections that Georgia worked with as a conservator at the NGV gave her a lot of creative fuel. Encountering significant pottery from around the world, and from the thousands of years during which ceramics have been produced, including Persian, Pre-Columbian, and Korean examples, as well as remarkable Australian examples from the 20th century, was a fantastic education. Working alongside these remarkable pieces, studying them technically and having the opportunity to handle them switched Georgia on to the possibilities that ceramics have to offer.

Unlike many of her contemporaries, Georgia expresses a detachment from her work, stating that the value lies in the process. While she is interested in how things turn out, and obviously exalted by her success – Georgia can part with pieces quite readily and is always looking to the next project. 'I only have a handful of pieces that I particularly want to hold on to. So although I have had my fair share of mishaps, none have been particularly disastrous – in fact the discoveries made through accidents are quite enlightening,' she says. 'I still feel the same excitement every day I settle in for a session in the studio. I also feel quite lucky to have come to ceramics during a period of growth and popular interest in the field.'

Above: Georgia's pieces often feature textures, rounded forms and vibrant colours.
Opposite: Georgia working on a new piece in her studio.
Following page, left: Georgia uses small electric kilns to fire her work at home.
Following page, right: Georgia uses a variety of techniques to create interesting
textures on her pieces, so that they appeal to multiple senses.

'The plasticity of clay is
the perfect vehicle –
so much can be conveyed
with a jaunty curve.'

loft

Giselle Hicks

The quality and sensibility that Giselle Hicks has been looking for in her work and studio practice relate to the ease and simplicity of her lifestyle in Montana. For many years her work and processes were rather complicated, involving a lot of steps, technical skill, knowledge and material. By the time she finished a piece, she felt it was suffocated, overworked and overwrought. 'I started making the pinch pots in response to the frustration with this other work. I wanted to make something with a process that was as simple and direct as possible,' she says.

Giselle has achieved that simplicity, creating work that has the fresh and dynamic aesthetic she desires, as well as experiencing that feeling in her working process. 'I use a commercial cone 6 porcelain and pinch the pots using only a banding wheel, hand-rolled coils, a fork to score a seam and a knife to cut an edge for a transition. That's it for tools and the technique is as basic as it gets,' she explains. 'My goal is to create forms that explore volume, proportion, posture, shape and colour. The qualities I was and am still looking for are generosity, stability, slowness, softness, simplicity and beauty.'

Giselle has been practising ceramics for fifteen years, earning both her Bachelor and Masters of Fine Arts in ceramics. The choice to work in clay was a holistic one, as she liked the material, the people around it, the history and the lifestyle it provided. She was always fascinated by the anthropology and the fact that there is a ceramics tradition pretty much anywhere you go in the world, so ceramics presented a way for her to learn about different cultural histories and traditions. On a practical level, she felt that the medium was pliable and incredibly versatile, that she would never get bored, given there is so much to learn both technically and conceptually. Giselle also liked that potters tend to be communal, often choosing to eat together, and sharing studio space, equipment and recipes. But possibly what left the strongest impression on her was her undergraduate professor and his wife, who always had their doors open to students for meals and to share their collection. 'This was the first time I saw what it was like to live in a house full of handmade objects. Everything in their house had a story. Their home was very alive, very rich. I wanted to be a part of that,' she recalls.

Finding it hard to distil a particular source for her creative inspiration, Giselle contends that she finds it in myriad forms. 'I look at Japanese pots, Scandinavian pots, basketry, architecture, textiles, my studio neighbour, contemporary sculpture, modernist painting and literature. It's all over the place.'

Echoing the sentiments of many potters, Giselle loves the way clay feels, the way it yields or responds to her body and touch. 'It makes me feel strong. I love that my body is tired and has been used after a long day in the studio,' she says.

CLAY

'I value the lifestyle of making and living with handmade things. I love the stories that these objects tell ... When I open my cupboards, I see my friends, mentors and all the places I've travelled.'

Previous page: Giselle aims for simplicity in all her work.
Above: Giselle uses a knife to cut shapes from greenware bodies.
Opposite: Giselle creates forms that explore volume, proportion, posture, shape and colour, using only pinching and coiling techniques.

Guy Van Leemput

Guy Van Leemput's original life path did not include clay. He studied mathematics at university, became a teacher, married, built a house and had three children. But then, when he was thirty-five, his best friend became very sick and died, a tragic event that acted as a catalyst for serious change.

Earlier, when Guy was preparing to go to university, he went to a neighbourhood potter and asked if he could help him without pay, 'just to learn things'. The potter agreed, and Guy spent three months helping in his studio. Even when university started he continued to help out in his spare time. He had a very genuine interest, though it was subjugated due to other more pressing commitments. But when his friend died, his priorities were re-ordered. 'That was the moment I decided not to dream of ceramics any longer but to do it. I took good tuition and attended master classes. Then I began to work with clay intensively. I have had my own workshop now for five years,' says Guy. 'For me ceramics is much more than a choice. I do not have the feeling that it came onto my path; it was more something I could not avoid. It is very difficult to know why I am attracted so strongly to ceramics. Perhaps it is about taking risks and letting go, hoping the kiln is doing its best for you? Perhaps it is about earth and fire, very simple but also very complex at the same time? Anyway, the "ceramic world" is such a nice world and it will stay my first love forever.'

Guy admits that he really only thinks about his work after he has finished, preferring working methods that allow him to stop thinking. 'I do not make any preliminary drawings, nor do I spend much time thinking about a form or a pattern. I just start working from images that are stored in me and the experience of previous work,' he explains. 'The stomach dictates the form, but the head makes the decisions. Each piece reflects my own self, and the better I get to know myself, the more profoundly I can proceed with my work. Thus each work becomes an investigation.'

In recent years, Guy has mainly worked with white porcelain, inventing a 'balloon technique' that allows him to make very thin translucent porcelain bowls. 'I start by blowing up a balloon, then I take porcelain reinforced with flax. I work directly on the balloon, starting at the bottom of the future bowl. First, I apply a small piece of porcelain with my stamp on it, and then add little cells one by one by manipulating the porcelain with small wooden tools, trying to not touch it too much with my hands. I can add only a small part each day,' he says.

Left: Guy applies a layer of porcelain slip to the inside of his pieces.

Each piece takes time – sometimes up to a month – after which Guy must be sure that the piece has dried evenly. After a few days he is then able to deflate the balloon, and coat the inside with a layer of porcelain slip. 'As my bowls are fired upside down to counteract the effects of gravity and the melting process at high temperature, I have to make a support for each piece. The piece is raw fired (once fired) in a wood kiln at 1300°C. I can fire this kiln very fast – after one hour of warming up, I go from 150°C to 1300°C in three to four hours. This high temperature is needed for strength and translucency. The wood firing gives the bowl a beautiful white colour and a sparkling blossom of glaze from ash deposits,' he explains.

In the summer of 2014, Guy was invited to be an artist in residence in Jingdezhen, China, and since then has been inspired to introduce colour into his work.

'For this series of translucent bowls I found inspiration in ancient Italian fresco paintings, both in colour and technique. Using stains for colouring the kaolin, and using these coloured slabs to roll into the walls of the bowl, inside and outside, achieves the same freshness in colour. The pattern on the inside interferes with the pattern on the outside, depending on the amount of light falling on the pot. Thus the spectacle changes during the day and the seasons,' he says.

When teaching future ceramicists, Guy always tells them to search for silence so they can listen to their hearts. And he always says that is only by following their own voice that they will find true satisfaction in their making.

Above and opposite: Guy doesn't plan forms or patterns in advance,
but lets them come naturally as he works.

'I can learn so much from a
stone or a branch, a pine cone
or a piece of burnt wood, a
beautiful pattern on a fish or
an egg, the rippling of water. '

Hannah Lawrence

Above: All of Hannah's pots are made using the pinching technique.

Hannah Lawrence was born in Cornwall. She studied art but decided that it wasn't for her, so in 2007 she travelled to Australia and spent time working on the land. This took the form of dwelling in communes, where people lived a subsistence lifestyle – growing their own food, building eco-houses, preparing meals and learning about people in a way that they don't teach you at school. 'I was greatly inspired by meeting people who were living off the land, and it helped me to see that my main focus was utility,' she says.

During this time, Hannah met two potters who introduced her to clay. 'Luckily I met the right people at the right time, as I had no formal training and spent the first few years almost entirely self-taught. I also found many incredible informal teachers along the way,' she recalls.

A most pertinent meeting was with potter Neil Hoffmann in Tasmania, a wood firer whose lifestyle Hannah felt was much in line with her own. Neil and his partner lived on 200 acres of eucalyptus forest, and allowed Hannah to stay for as long as she wanted. 'Neil has eight different wood kilns and an endless supply of eucalyptus wood, lots of clay and glaze materials and an extremely generous heart! I learnt so much during that time with him, it really changed my life,' says Hannah. 'For me, my relationship with ceramics is self-exploratory. I think people achieve this exploration through many different mediums, but for me clay is the perfect way to delve deeply into process and practice. The rewards feel very directly linked to how much one puts in. When you're immersed in your practice you learn a great deal very quickly.'

A few years later, Hannah was travelling in Japan and undertook an impromptu five-day wood-firing course with a small group of Japanese potters in Shikoku. 'It was another very lucky meeting that really left a lasting impression on me. I couldn't speak much Japanese, and they couldn't speak any English, but we formed an amazing bond just through our shared love of pottery and nature.' Now back in Cornwall, Hannah runs Folklore, a small independent craft shop selling her own ceramics, plus a variety of handcrafted

objects such as woodwork, basketry and clothing, with the aim to promote Cornish craft that is both functional and beautiful.

Hannah uses mostly stoneware clay, and sometimes porcelain, gas fired to 1300°C. 'I am a pinch potter and use minimal tools. I mix all my own glazes and the recipes are simple and natural, and all my glazes include wood ash. I think my style is natural and without strained effort,' Hannah says. 'The pots are generally small and quiet with both the form and surface non-uniform, but subtle.'

Hannah is most proud of her teapots. 'Firstly because I find them very beautiful, and secondly because making teapots using the pinching technique is pretty difficult and time consuming!'

Finding inspiration from the very primitive and ancient pottery of England, India, Egypt, Africa and Japan, Claire is drawn to their raw simplicity and boldness. 'I particularly love the anonymous ancient Egyptian pots in the British Museum near the downstairs toilet! They are all small, unglazed and shockingly simple. Without doubt the most beautiful pots I have ever seen,' she shares.

Holly Macdonald

Holly Macdonald says that the clues to her future ceramics career were there all along – eating pancakes from plates handmade by her mother in the 1970s, pottery classes as a ten-year-old with her siblings, and working with clay in high school – although she wasn't consciously thinking of all these things when she made that first decision to embark on a Bachelor of Fine Arts in ceramics at the National Art School Sydney in 2012. 'There has always been a familiarity with the medium. Working with clay creates a feeling of connectedness – quite literally – through physical engagement. But it works on an intellectual and emotional level for me, too,' she explains.

It is the expressive possibilities in clay that Holly finds so alluring, and the strong personality of the medium. 'There is a tension between the plastic and earth-bound nature of clay and my desire to control it. It is a collaborative effort between the maker and the clay and other ceramic materials being used to get the work to where you want it,' she describes.

Holly's work is colourful, intuitive and playful. She treats the ceramic vessel as a canvas, engaging both the internal and external surfaces to hold and direct her abstract drawings. 'The drawn element begins as sketches in a journal. I'm sketching all the time, things that I have noticed and remembered from urban and natural environments,' she says. 'I like to think that my studio is in my head and in my hands and I can transport that anywhere. But a needle tool, a paring knife and a banding wheel also come in handy.'

Favouring hand building in clay, Holly tends to work in porcelain but also uses terracotta or raku clay. Her sketches are then translated onto the clay surface freehand and in layers throughout the making process, with the slip and stain applied at the leather-hard stage. At the bisque stage she will start to draw with ceramic crayons and pencils, and continue to apply glaze and engobe. 'Sometimes the creative process is compromised because the clay has its own time line. For example the raw clay form might dry out and so then I might not be able to inlay slip ... often I will try anyway though. I like seeing how far I can push the medium,' says Holly.

Holly views her own ceramics work as tied up with a long human history. For her, it is a means of communicating with and understanding the world around us. She admires the part that pottery plays in preserving information about the way different cultures stored and transported goods, and the way they gathered to share food, as well as its part in

Left: Holly at work on the banding wheel.

ceremony and tradition. Holly sees the role of the ceramic vessel has long been a vehicle for storytelling, with folk tales and religious stories being painted onto and inscribed into the clay surface. 'And I guess it is also about our relationship with the land and our feelings of ownership over it. What we find in the ground, like clay or like coal, is taken as ours to mine and transform. Clay already has many meanings attached to it, which is an important part of the attraction,' she explains.

The inherent disasters that are inevitable in a ceramics practice is something about which Holly remains philosophical, stating that you do get used to things breaking and smashing as part and parcel of the medium. 'Its fragility is possibly part of the appeal,' she says. 'There are certainly a lot of opportunities to practise non-attachment in working with clay. Non-attachment in relation to the physical things you are creating and the expectations you have of them. I think it's a good thing, and is a positive influence on other areas of my life.'

Above: Holly sketches her designs in a journal first,
then paints them freehand onto the clay.
Opposite: Holly prefers hand building to throwing.

'I love cracking open the kiln door after glaze firing to see that everything is still standing! These moments are pure joy.'

Jeremy Simons

Above and opposite: Jeremy's works are one-off pieces inspired by natural forms and textures.

Jeremy Simons suggests that his state of mind determines the outcome of his ceramic forms. He also believes that weather, sounds, mood and music all play a role in his creative process. 'Any session in the studio is determined by different feelings and methods of working and thereby produces different shapes, forms or textures. The challenge for me is keeping continuity within a body of work,' he explains. Jeremy makes, throws or builds as often as time permits, describing his love of the process – and its inherent meditative state – as much as the works themselves.

Jeremy's introduction to ceramics started when he was at high school, and he was inspired to further his studies while doing a visual arts degree at Sydney College of the Arts. Graduating with a Bachelor of Visual Arts in 1998 with a double major in ceramics and photography, he has been making ceramic works and using clay in one way or another ever since. While it was photography that he chose to pursue on a professional level, Jeremy has reinvigorated his passion and love for clay over the last four years. 'I'm not exactly sure if photography informs my ceramics, but maybe it does? I chose to reimmerse myself back into clay as a medium because it allows me a different creative freedom. It's not my nine-to-five job, it's my creative passion,' he explains.

What Jeremy enjoys is that clay allows him to work in a free-form way, where ideas and concepts can flow. The outcome is undetermined and solely driven by himself and his state of being, with no deadline, no team to confer with, no brief to follow nor client to please. 'I suppose more than anything I'm looking for that balance between both mediums, but for now I'm happy to keep them separate … as they've both played an equal role in my life so far,' he says.

Jeremy usually sets aside whole weekends to be with clay, throwing and making on Saturday, finishing and turning on Sunday, followed by another weekend of glazing and testing, and then another firing. No free time goes unused. Inspired by the earth, found materials and natural textures, he creates one-off pieces using a range of techniques and methods, including earth firings

incorporating sawdust, animal bone, seaweed and ochre to establish
an organic and textural working method. 'I use a range of clays but
most commonly stoneware and a raku-based clay. My textures
usually derive from nature, palm husk, coral, bone, hessian and
tree resin. Specific works are re-fired in earth kilns using seaweed,
sawdust and dung to finish unique one-off forms. With this method
there is little control over the outcome,' he says.

Ceramicists are told many times over to never get attached to
a piece until it's out of the final firing, but it's a long, hard lesson
to learn. 'Using earth firings and barrel kilns brings a high percentage
of breakages and cracking due to falling logs and thermal shock.
Opening a kiln post-firing can be the happiest of days – or the
saddest,' Jeremy admits.

What clay does represent to Jeremy is a freedom to create, and a
material without limits – where the process of making is the journey
during which he finds new paths and inspiration.

Above and opposite: Jeremy's aesthetic is natural and earthy.
He uses a variety of techniques to create texture in his work.

'When I come out from a
session in my studio I have
to readjust to the outside
world, reconnect with
others and family, and then
return to the studio later
to reassess my form.'

Jessilla Rogers

Jessilla Rogers aims to make ceramics that capture the feeling of a long, hot Australian summer spent at the beach or swimming at the pool under an infinite blue sky. She is particularly interested in colour and pattern, and these have fast become hallmarks of her work. 'My work is very painterly, kind of wonky and perhaps naïve, I suppose. It's been called childlike – and I don't know how I feel about that description! Making childlike-looking work is not my intention,' Jessilla explains.

Jessilla's work is her own take on regal or ancient ceramic forms, and she often visits galleries or researches ceramics via the internet. 'It's a chance for me to make things that are normally only owned by royalty or live in museums. However, in my studio I make my own versions of these things and then they exist for me or for others as versions of these grand objects. It's like a democratization of sorts,' she says. 'Ceramics represents a way of making everyday art, objects that become a part of your life. I have this image where you are sitting down for a dinner party and the company is great, the food's delicious and the wine is beautiful – and my ceramics just slot into that scene and complete the picture. I once titled a piece *This Must be the Place*; that scene I just described, that is that place.'

For Jessilla, ceramics also affords her a lifestyle whereby she feels privileged to get up every day and go to her studio to make the things that she has dreamt up, and then share those things with other people and see what they do with them.

Graduating with an arts degree with an art history major, Jessilla planned to do a masters in curating. 'But I had always loved making things, making art, and had wanted to go to art school,' she says. 'The thought of curating other people's work made me feel really envious of the artists!'

After finishing her degree, Jessilla went to Japan for six months and reflected on what she would do when she returned to Australia. She had been going to casual pottery classes at a studio near her home while she was studying, so when she got home she started going there again to build up a portfolio to apply for university. She successfully gained a place studying ceramics at RMIT. 'It was really great, as I learned how to make glazes and how to fire in gas kilns, but I was also picking up stockists, and being asked to be involved in exhibitions, and getting orders for my work. As a result, I never actually finished my course,' says Jessilla.

Now, after making ceramics for eight years, her advice is simple. 'Only make the things you want to

Left: Jessilla feels privileged that she can spend time in her studio every day.

make, not what you think other people will like,' says Jessilla. 'You'll lose interest otherwise, and you won't be able to sustain your practice because you'll run out of ideas. I think I'm most proud that to date I've only ever made things I've wanted to make and that people have been OK with that and they have trusted me enough to allow me that freedom.'

In her practice, Jessilla always fires to stoneware temperatures. She admits may be considered curious because traditionally earthenware is so synonymous with colours, but she likes the strength and durability of stoneware. Jessilla employs both wheel throwing and hand building, typically adding hand-built elements to her wheel-thrown pieces. She glazes her work with a base colour, and then paints over the glaze before firing, sometimes adding a third lustre firing.

What Jessilla loves most are the surprises inherent in her craft. 'I put something in the kiln, hope for the best and then am often pleasantly surprised by the results. There's a degree of control that you have but you can never make exactly the same thing twice. There is always variation and I like that. It means you can't be too precious or hold things too close.'

Above and opposite: Colour and pattern are signatures of Jessilla's work.
[Yellow piece in centre of collection by Tessy King.]

'My work is inspired by an amalgamation of all my favourite books, films, artworks, places I've been and things I've seen.'

Jono Smart

While working in a high-end garden design studio, Jono Smart was fortunate enough to have the kind of budgets that meant everything that went into his gardens was handmade. This brought him into contact with many different artisans, such as stonemasons, metalworkers, plant growers and carpenters, and he always felt the pangs of longing when he visited them. 'As a designer I would have the initial idea, but the making was done by other people. I was aware of the gap this left in my understanding. Designing gave me a great overview of many materials, but nothing in-depth,' he says.

To appease his longing to make, Jono took up a few crafts as hobbies, such as silversmithing, carpentry and pottery. He also started collecting pottery from his favourite makers across the world, including Kirstie van Noort, Takashi Endo and Billy Lloyd. 'I spent a lot of time researching ceramics and was fortunate to visit Julian Stair's studio. I actually couldn't wait to make my own.'

As a garden designer, Jono created minimal gardens, concentrating on straight lines, texture and repetition, and this has had a major effect on his ceramics work. He was taught that a designer's work doesn't start when you enter your studio in the morning; rather it is how you live your life, the care you take over cooking, the books you choose to read, the places and people you visit. This all becomes you and you become your designs.

In early 2014, Jono joined an open communal studio in East London and was tutored in the fundamentals by Stuart Carey. It was this mentorship that allowed him to become the full-time ceramicist that he is today.

Jono's work is deliberately simple. His forms are basic, almost rudimentary, with straight, unbroken lines and gestures of tapering or flaring. 'The forms are canvasses for me to test surfaces and glaze finishes. Blacks, greys, whites and stone make up my palette of colours. I'm looking for gentle, natural colours that can be part of daily life rather than statement work,' he describes. Jono has cut the number of clays he uses in his studio down to three stoneware clays, and he uses them to create seven or eight different finishes by adding various oxides, stains and sand directly into the clay to create different colours and textures. The oxide is measured to the nearest 0.01 per cent and he wedges it into the clay before throwing it, and finally uses simple clear, white and grey glazes to line the interior of each piece. 'With most of my work I leave the

Left: Jono experiments with blended clay bodies, and codes his mixtures to help him remember the various recipes he used to create different colours and textures.

exterior of the piece unglazed, showing the clay in its raw fired state. This gives each piece a matte, tactile feel. People want to handle the pieces,' he explains.

Many of Jono's pieces have a minimal tab handle that has become a recognizable feature of his work. 'At first glance, most people are not sure of its function and think it's a simple decorative addition, but the handle creates a small, comfortable lever for the hand. It sits above the knuckle of your forefinger as you're drinking, stabilizing your hand.'

Jono feels that the very best potters – and the best designers in any chosen field – are those who can express themselves most clearly. 'To have something expressed with clarity in an object that you can use feels very human. I feel like I understand the person who made each piece in a way that I couldn't by just talking with them.'

Jono describes the satisfaction that can be derived from a solo ceramics practice. 'If I was an architect I would need the culmination of the right client, the right space and the right budget all at the same time to express my ideas. And even then it would take many people working together to create this idea in reality. The only limits are my skill and my effort,' he says. 'This makes my work feel limitless.'

The interconnected digital world of social media, while light years away from the simple tactility of clay, has fostered direct contact and a conversation with an audience, which Jono enjoys. 'It is just a gift to current makers. It's like having a daily exhibition. If I am able to connect images and words together to share my experience of making, then people across the world give me their time and attention, I can't ask for any more than that.'

Above and opposite: Jono's signature tab handles have become
a hallmark of his work.

'There aren't many moments in our day-to-day lives when we use something handmade. I use many other potters' work in my life, and I love the care and thought each of them has put into it.'

Above and opposite: Jono's forms are deliberately simple, with a restricted colour palette of blacks, greys, whites and stone.

Julie Pennington

Being able to transform a solid, heavy block of clay into light, delicate objects that appear fragile, yet are in fact strong, is Julie Pennington's creative *raison d'être*. Striving to evoke a feeling of fragility and quietness in her work, Julie makes pieces that are characterized by intricate porcelain elements, which explore form, pattern and texture. Line, and the use of positive and negative space, feature prominently in both her vessel forms and her sculptural pieces.

'My current practice focuses on hand building, and I work in a fairly intuitive way, allowing the making process to inform my practice,' she explains. 'I use porcelain, enjoying its working qualities, as well as the whiteness and translucency it offers.'

Pattern and texture have heavily influenced Julie's work in all its forms. She draws inspiration from the natural environment, contemporary basketry and weaving, as well as architectural detail like ironwork, stone and brick. 'My early involvement in drawing, printmaking and textiles has also informed my work. Mark making and the power of the line continue to be of interest to me, whether this be in two-dimensional or three-dimensional work,' says Julie.

Julie's process begins with finely rolled, often textured coils. When making vessel forms, she doesn't blend the coils together as is usually the procedure, but lets them remain evident as a surface texture. Julie also uses coils to construct elaborate structures, which is done in stages to allow sections to firm up before proceeding further. These works are usually made on clay formers or directly onto a kiln shelf due to their fragility, and then high-fired in oxidation in an electric kiln. 'My work also incorporates small hand-formed components, and textures made from found objects, linocuts and stamps. I use very little glaze, sometimes just some clear glaze to highlight and catch the light,' she says.

Despite an earlier career in education, there was always an underlying interest and engagement in art and art making. 'My parents were creative so there were art materials and art books around as I was growing up. My decision to change career paths started with study and work in the field of textile design,' she explains. Around this same time there were a lot of hobby ceramic studios opening up, and Julie was encouraged by a friend to try some of her designs on pots. Enjoying the process of designing for three-dimensional forms, she eventually decided that she wanted to start making her own pots from scratch rather than buying greenware. This coincided

Left: Inspired by basketry and weaving, Julie uses coils to hand build her vessels.

with a move from the city to a more rural part of Australia, where Julie enrolled in a ceramics course at the vocational education provider TAFE. 'I started this course about 15 years ago, and went on at a later stage to do a diploma in ceramics. It is really only in the last five years or so that I have been able to dedicate time to building my ceramics practice,' she explains. 'Starting a career in ceramics later in life can be frustrating, pondering where you might be if only you had started sooner!'

While she admits that working from a home studio has a lot of positives, Julie is also honest about the trials. 'It can be challenging in terms of time management, and also being taken seriously by others. It can feel very isolated. Marketing one's work, gaining recognition and making a living from ceramics are all very time-consuming and challenging aspects of being

an artist! I have recently embraced Instagram, and this has helped me enormously to feel part of the ceramics community!' she shares. On the topic of social media, Julie's advice is loud and clear. 'Get out there and get noticed! Try not to get too side-tracked by fashion; stay focused on what is meaningful to you.'

Julie believes that the current buoyancy and interest in ceramics is tied to a greater desire for a unique and sustainable product. 'Buyers are seeking out ways to connect with the maker, and they have an appetite for knowing who made something, how it was made and where the materials come from. Social media, markets and design fairs have helped people to make these connections with artists, which is a great thing for everyone.'

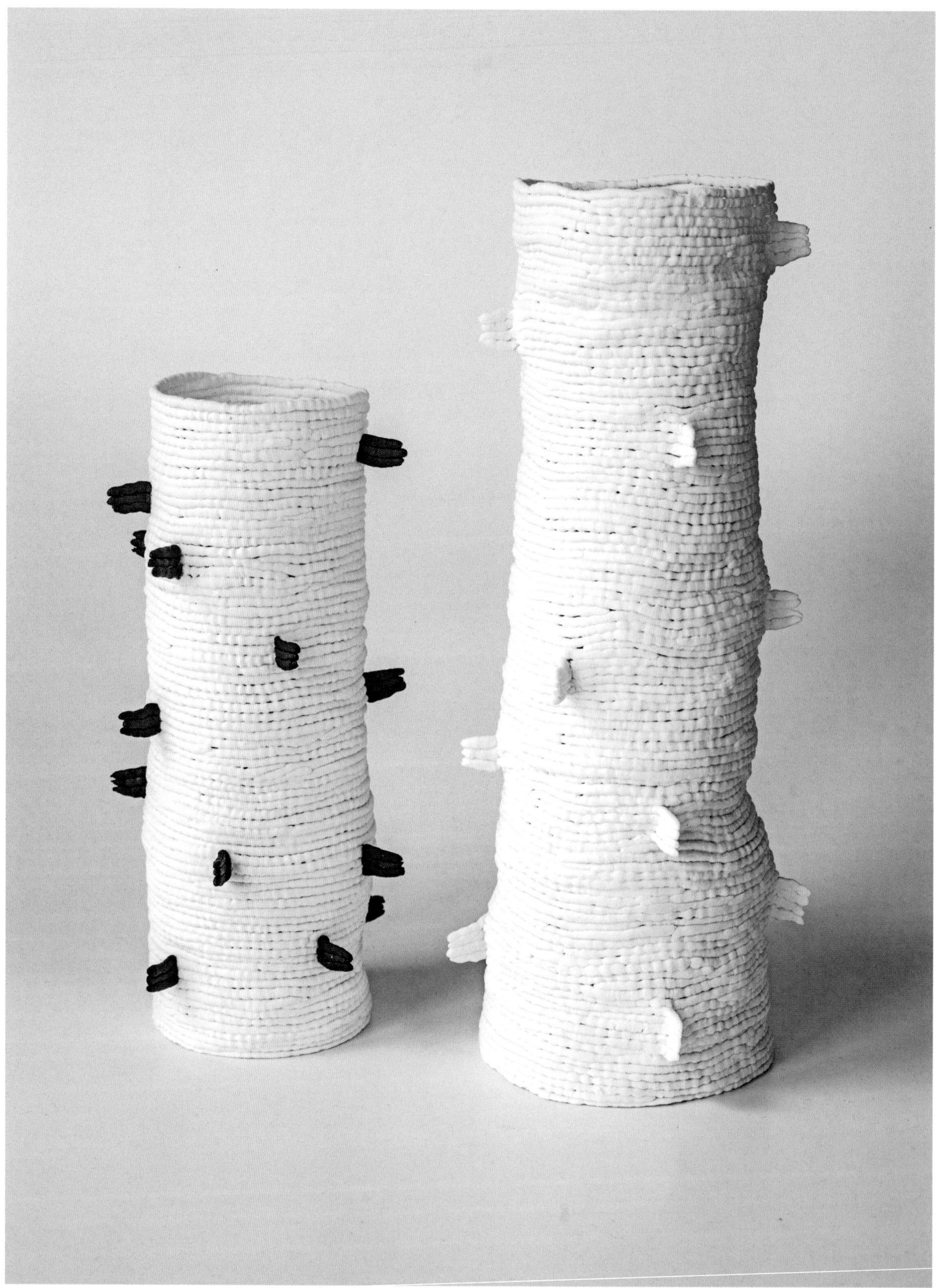

CLAY

'The exciting thing about ceramics is that it can be so many things. You have people making beautiful domestic ware, right through to thought-provoking installation works. The possibilities are endless!'

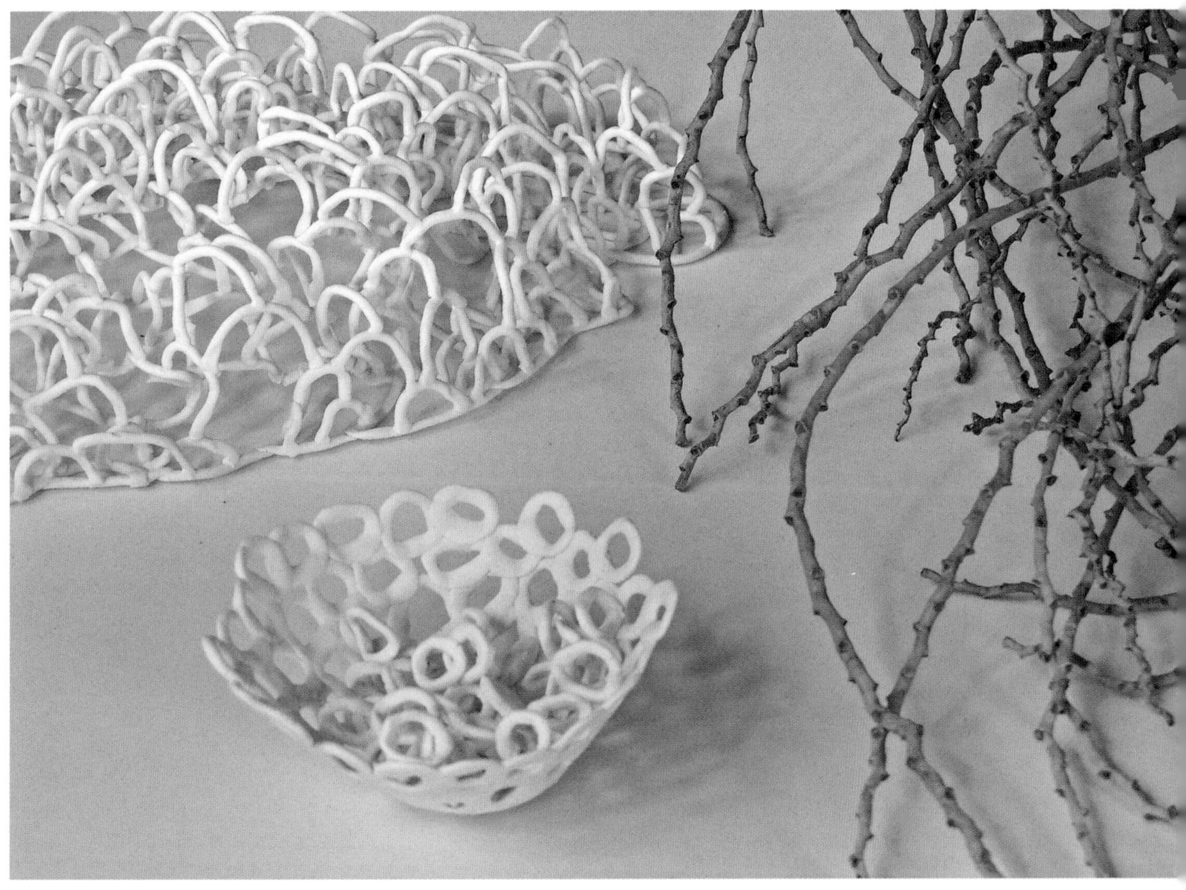

Above: Julie often makes these pieces directly onto the kiln shelf because they are so fragile.
Opposite: Rather than blending coils together, Julie leaves them to provide surface texture.

Katia Carletti

Katia Carletti describes working with clay as a way to calm and focus her brain. She is at her most contented when slowly and methodically working to create new forms. 'I love that functional pottery can be beautiful as well as practical, a way to really take notice of and celebrate everyday rituals,' she says.

Katia trained as a painter at art school, but she stumbled upon ceramics as a way to bring her paintings into the three-dimensional world. 'I was making work about everyday rituals, but soon I didn't want to just make work that was "about" those ideas, I wanted them to actually be.' Katia explains that it slowly dawned on her that, 'All I wanted to do was make little cups and things that I could use myself to eat from and arrange on shelves.' She has now been working seriously with clay for over two years.

As someone who didn't study ceramics at art school, Katie has found that probably the biggest influence on her practice has been time itself. She considers her way of learning as subconscious, preferring to visualize a shape and then work out the practicalities of making it with her hands. 'The last couple of years working with clay, teaching myself, has been all about just pushing things around, seeing what happens when I try different things, what the limitations and possibilities of hand building can be,' she says. 'Hand building is very intuitive, and lends itself to slow shifts in style. Lots of my current work has carved patterns. At first I had just one carved design, but slowly over time I realized that I could use different tools and formations to create lots of different forms! I think I get bored pretty easily, so I'm always testing new things out. This probably comes from my art background rather than a more structured "studio craft" way of learning.' Katia's works also evolve from looking widely, finding inspiration from nature, patterns in textiles, as well as her own desires for certain ceramics in the kitchen.

Making all of her work using a hand-built, pinched technique, Katia is interested in creating forms that are practical, feel nice to hold, and speak to one another through tone and subtle pattern. Her methods involve using either high-fired stoneware fired in a reduction atmosphere, or porcelain fired in oxidation. Many of her pieces are embellished with carved patterns or facets, small handles, or geometric painted designs in monochromatic tones. Katia says her greatest love is making things that are both practical and special, and can be used every day. 'Fitting a lid onto a canister and finding that it fits perfectly, testing a teapot and seeing that it has a perfect pour, opening a glaze kiln and seeing that everything survived, spending a lovely long day in the studio and just having a nice time experimenting with different shapes ... these are the joys of my practice,' she affirms.

Previous page: Katia hand builds her pieces using the pinching technique.
Above and opposite: Stoneware vessels showing contrast between dark
stoneware clay and porcelain with the same speckle glaze.

Katie Jacobs

As a child, Katie Jacobs always wanted to be an inventor. She reflects that, at the heart of it, many of us use our sense of touch as a way of understanding the physical world. 'The life of an artist is always inventing new things, in a lot of cases without the restriction of function!' she says.

Katie graduated from Monash University in Melbourne in 2002 with a Bachelor of Applied Arts (Ceramics) with Honours, the recipient of a Dean's Scholarship Program Full Academic Scholarship. This was followed by the completion of her Master of Fine Arts (Ceramics) in 2014 at Indiana University in the USA. Having now worked with clay for twenty years (including high school), she believes that clay ultimately chose her. 'If I don't touch clay for a while, I actually get frustrated and pretty grumpy. Clay is cheaper than heroin or therapy. Fact.'

Animals are consistent themes in Katie's work, particularly Australian natives such as kangaroos and Leadbeater's possums, as well as her dog Lillie. 'Also, objects that I view as icons, in the tradition of excellent pop artist Claes Oldenburg – a wolf head T-shirt, sports balls, leopard print worn by David Lee Roth, and Frankenstein's monster,' she explains. 'I like wooing people with craft skills, aesthetic pop imagery and humour to distract from bigger concepts in work about the vulnerability, seriousness and silliness of the human condition. I like to think of my pieces as romantically naïve, often "cute", sometimes a little bit lumpy, often inspired by folk art, hopefully expressive of a dark humour – but I'd probably prefer others to describe the style as they see it!' she says. 'I think my style constantly evolves, but I'd say that narrative and concept drive my practice, so I use materials and clay as the project demands.'

On a residency in Denmark, Katie made a sculpture of Princess Mary with the idea that it was about the perfect princess 'icon' story. 'So I made this perfect white clay skin using that factory-produced slip-casting technique, with European classic blue–white coloured porcelain. But sanding it made carbon come off the sandpaper causing black spots to appear on the nose and forehead, which I was pretty annoyed about,' she recalls. Some of her ceramics friends were there to suggest re-firing in an oxidation atmosphere, and the marks did come out again. 'Unfortunately at an exhibition I had to show the freckled version, which I was upset about at the time. But it really was not such a big problem, as I thought the freckles looked quite sweet! Things go wrong or break all the time, but if you

Left: Animal forms feature
heavily in Katie's work.

get upset about it, you couldn't be a ceramicist!' she acknowledges with a rueful smile.

Katie embraces any and all of the ceramic materials and techniques that she can get her hands on. 'As a teacher or parent, you are not meant to have favourites, but currently my favourite "child" is big hand building, with chunky grog and red iron-rich clay. I like the challenge, and the risk that a large sculpture might fail, and the fact that you can disguise coils with texture to show off some old-school craft skill.'

For Katie, working with clay is about human touch. 'I love physically touching it, and it records that touch at a moment in time, which is tremendous. It also brings about human connections and draws me to so many others who also love it.' Katie is fortunate enough that her career with clay has taken her around the world and given her the opportunity to learn from her fellow ceramicists in America, Canada, Denmark and New Zealand.

Katie explains that for her it is crucial to share technical knowledge, as it is such a large and significant part of the process. 'This is one thing that draws me to ceramics, as a social and craft information-sharing community,' she says. She is also a big fan of collaboration, finding conversations with fellow artists about work they are doing together are often inspirational and get her to the true heart of the idea. 'I find working with other people can make your work and your concepts so much better. Getting in the zone in the studio is nice, and coming out of it with a new piece is a fantastic feeling. Exhibiting is a great chance to stand back from your work and see if you are doing what you intended.'

Above and opposite: Katie uses familiar imagery in her work, such as sports balls and animal forms.

‘I desperately try to include humour in all my works. People are so much more open to ideas when they are laughing.’

Keiko Matsui

Above: Keiko's work is very personal, as she allows her emotions to influence what she creates.

Keiko Matsui works predominately in porcelain. Her work begins on the potter's wheel and is then manipulated, cut and reassembled to evoke a quiet and subtle abstraction. Making and reinterpreting objects is her focus, and she pays particular attention to the form, proportion and profile of a vessel, as well as the interconnectedness between the interior and exterior.

Keiko describes how she always listens to her feelings carefully, and this intuition informs her practice, with her feelings and experiences undeniably manifesting in her work. Illustrative of the very personal and subjective nature of Keiko's work is *Torn*, a grouping of ten unglazed vessels that were ripped at the rim, made right after the complicated birth of her son in 2011. A year later, she made sculptural vessels called *Mother and Child* that are more curved in form, with a softer, white glaze. 'I feel that my work is constantly changing and I think that small things and events in my everyday life are influencing both me as a person and also my ceramics work,' she describes.

Born in Japan, Keiko found that life in busy cities like Osaka and Tokyo quelled a creative career. Growing up, she was interested in all sorts of creative making but found that living in such harried cities did not allow her time to stop and think about what she wanted to do. Keiko eventually found her passion in clay when she moved to Australia seventeen years ago. 'Living in Australia gave me the opportunity to find my real voice. The lifestyle is slow here compared to Japan. There is beautiful nature and spaces and many different cultures in Australia. Being surrounded by this rich environment has enabled me to focus on what I really want to pursue in my life,' she says.

Keiko's work is simple and free in form and glaze. It bears an obvious Japanese aesthetic from her early upbringing, with influence from her new antipodean life. 'My blue and white pieces are my signature work, as this was the first work I created at the National Art School in Sydney. Now I am inclined more towards minimal designs such as my scar vessels,' explains Keiko. Keiko's 'scar' vessels are a

Above: Keiko's vessels explore the connections between the interior and exterior.

series of functional porcelain objects made on the potter's wheel and cut and re-joined with textured slurry on the rim. The name is derived from the joined parts which can resemble human scars — a very visceral technique rich in metaphor.

Keiko's recent work explores the kintsugi technique: the Japanese art of repairing broken ceramics with lacquer dusted or mixed with powdered gold, silver or platinum. This is something she hopes to continue to explore and practise. 'I am also interested in the relationship between vessels and ikebana (flower arranging). I have been creating functional and sculptural vessels for a long time.'

What Keiko loves most is the mental solace she finds at the potter's wheel. While she admits that there are ever-present challenges on the technical side, these can always be solved. The most difficult aspect is emptying her head and keeping up her work every day. 'I have found that it is very hard to juggle motherhood and my practice. This may be because of my character ... when I concentrate on one thing, I cannot see the other thing!'

CLAY

'I often feel like
the clay is my
teacher – a teacher
who shows me
the important
things in life.'

Above and opposite: Keiko's work is influenced by the Japanese art of ikebana, or flower arranging.

Kira Ni

Latvian-born Kira Ni's ceramics journey began in London, though she is now practising in Valletta, Malta, enjoying the inevitable influences that her surrounding environment has on her practice.

Driven by an overriding desire to help transform a house into a cosy, modern yet rustic home, Kira is influenced by the same intangible comforts one might find in the smell of freshly baked food, the softness of linen, the scent of meadow flowers and the warmth of a fireplace. It is her hope that when you hold a Kira Ni vase in your hand, you experience a feeling of placidity.

For Kira, ceramics provides an opportunity for non-verbal conversation through the pieces that she makes. 'Feelings and emotions that are too hard to put into words can be aptly expressed with clay,' she says. The core of her style comes from Scandinavian design, with a twist of rustic and the humble clean lines that encourage you to appreciate the inherent imperfection in handcrafted objects. 'My signature work is the *Seagull Jug*. I could reproduce this a million times and every time it would be different from the previous one, each of them with its own character,' says Kira.

Kira works with stoneware clay, using only three colours – black, white and grey – as well as two glaze colours, transparent and white. 'I see these colours as a canvas for the shapes that I am making. They don't "scream" but rather allow the shape to flow,' she explains. After starting off throwing on the potter's wheel, with time Kira shifted towards hand building. She finds it refreshing to change techniques occasionally, exploring clay's potential and pushing herself to create new shapes.

There is a self-belief to Kira that belies her short ceramics career. In January 2014, at the time on a corporate path, she spontaneously signed up for an evening pottery workshop – her first brush with clay. 'I don't really know how it happened exactly. It was like a spark ignited inside of me. I spent the next ten months attending the workshop and different classes. I started planning my brand and practising my skills.'

The rest happened very quickly. Kira left her job and put her corporate career on hold in the hope of creating something that she could feel was truly her own. Kira Ni Ceramics was launched in February 2015 and since then it has gone from strength to strength.

What Kira loves about ceramics is that it allows her to make structurally functional, and affordable, everyday pieces of art. She feels that she has come to the party at a time when ceramics and all things handmade are garnering a new appreciation. 'I love how people want to own a wonky ceramic bowl in their perfect, modern houses. And how you can now find pottery pieces in trendy fashion shops,' she explains. 'I feel very positive about this trend.'

There are of course challenges. Kira confides openly, 'Production is time-consuming, so at the end of the day I might not produce enough work to supply my stockists and make a profit as well as have enough to sell directly from my own website. So at the moment it is a bit of a learning curve.'

Kira has achieved much in a short time and is proud of the fact that she took the leap to become a full-time potter. Her work is now found in the United States, United Kingdom and Malta.

'I like to describe my style as quiet and simple. In this less-is-more way I find that each piece can be easily integrated into any design.'

CLAY

Above and opposite: Kira works with stoneware clay in black, white and grey only, and uses transparent or white glazes. The muted colour palette allows the form to speak for itself.

Linda Lopez

Growing up on a small farm in Visalia, California, Linda Lopez considers herself a late bloomer in art. The daughter of a Mexican immigrant father who worked as a farm hand and a Vietnamese refugee mother who worked in a kitchen, Linda grew up in the midst of a lush vegetable garden, with fruit trees and a cohort of farm animals. 'I loved spending time with my parents climbing hay bales, milking goats and picking fresh cherries off the trees, but I could not see a future in agriculture at the time,' she recollects.

It wasn't until Linda's third year of college that she decided to major in art. 'I went to my advisor at College of the Sequoias ready to transfer to a university. I had earned my AA in liberal arts leaning towards childhood development. I had no idea what my major would be and all of a sudden the options seemed endless. My advisor recommended an aptitude test to help narrow down the options, and the results indicated that I should be a farmer!' says Linda. But a farmer she was not meant to be. After a conversation with her advisor, Linda settled on art.

Linda transferred and moved straight into three studio courses and one art history course in her first semester at California State University, Chico. 'It was horrifying. I felt so out of my league. I had absolutely no experience making art, talking about art, or thinking about art. It was the most difficult semester of my academic career, but I was hooked,' she says. 'The most difficult course was ceramics. It was the most challenging conceptually and technically. I loved how you could make it into anything and hated how uncontrollable it could be. Ceramics and I have now been together since 2002.'

Linda's work is playful and abstract, and she is interested in making things that she does not quite understand. 'What influences my style? I find this question difficult to wrap language around. There is so much that influences my work, yet pinpointing each detail is hard. Everyday moments of wonder and confusion are certainly influential. These are things that intrigue me to look and see, things that make me stop and question what the object really is. The moments where something becomes unrecognizable and we question the things we think we understand. Can we recognize new things without the hindrances of what we have already learned?' she asks. Literature also informs her imagination. 'Haruki Murakami and Miranda July – how they write in mundane dreamscapes on the boundaries of what is real and what is not real inspires me.'

Clay plays a large role in Linda's practice, but she does not limit her materials, using what she feels the work needs – which can sometimes be fabric, drawings and, most recently, rugs. Linda describes clay as a material that can be anything, so it allows her to work intuitively and abstractly. Her ceramic practice focuses on hand building with low-fire clay. Linda coil builds all of her pieces and often includes nylon fibres to add strength to the linear pieces while in the greenware stage. 'I have most recently ventured into cone 6 porcelain. I love the flux in the surface and the slight sheen when fired to temperature. The glazes are also more saturated in hue on such a pure white surface,' she says.

Linda is most proud of the fact that she and her husband, ceramicist Mathew McConnell, are both still practising studio artists. 'In some ways, I feel like we, my husband and I, beat the odds. I feel so lucky to have a career in ceramics at this moment. The appetite and appreciation for ceramics have exploded in contemporary art,' she says.

Recalling a time when she was getting ready for a solo show, Linda shows how, in ceramics, variables outside your control are never far away. 'I was feeling good about the schedule and work until I opened a glaze kiln. I peered inside and everything had shivered. I had no idea why, since I was using a familiar clay and glaze recipe. I realized that one of the ingredients had changed in mining locations, which affected the compatibility of my clay and glaze! I was devastated, but luckily I had enough work to fulfil my exhibition.'

Above and opposite: Linda's work centres on abstract forms.

‘My advice is to be aware of
your contemporaries – and
work harder than them!’

Above and opposite: Working with cone 6 porcelain, Linda enjoys the glaze colour saturation that can be achieved on such a pure white surface.

Lucile Sciallano

Above: Lucile's studio in Brunswick.

French-born Lucile Sciallano, aka La Petite Fabrique de Brunswick, claims that luck and randomness often play a vital part in her process. The chance sighting of a shape or a line in nature or in a painting will spark an idea about what she could make. She also confesses to an innate trust in the ability of her own hands, without yielding to too much overthinking.

Lucile uses slip-cast porcelain to make functional wares, working with a limited palette of colours and always using a stain in the slip rather than coloured glazes. Although she is most widely recognized for her blue-and-white wares, each pattern she makes is unique, and she says that people are drawn to different designs. Working with a slip-casting porcelain called Imperial White, she first creates her prototype in plaster, clay or wood, then uses that to create her mould.

Originally completing a Bachelor in Object Design in France in 2011, Lucile was exposed to a way of teaching that hovered between design and art. A masters degree at the Design Academy Eindhoven in the Netherlands was to follow in 2013, where she learned how to combine research and making, essentially marrying her brain and her hands. 'That's where I fell in love with ceramics and even though I couldn't do all my projects in it, I knew that as soon as I graduated and could choose my medium that would be my focus. I like the versatility of clay – that it's a natural material, that there is a process to follow, and you can return to work on the object several times. I love playing with the rules of the medium, and try to push the boundaries to see what could work and not.'

When she arrived in Melbourne in December 2013, Lucile serendipitously moved into a house across the road from a pottery supply shop. It became clear that pursuing a ceramic practice was inevitable, and the garden shed at her new home soon became her studio space. 'When I started my studio, I found a very supportive community around craft and the handmade. Working by yourself can make you feel lonely, but here I got a lot of help and very good tips from other makers. That makes a big difference when you start your own studio,' she says.

Ceramics has now graduated from being a passion project to a bona fide business for Lucile. 'Even though starting your own business is really exciting and being able to do what you love for a living is bliss, sometimes it can be really hard and you can find yourself having doubts. If you don't push yourself to get out of bed every morning no one else will do it. So combined with moving over to the other side of the world, setting up my studio and trying to make it sustainable, it's an ever-evolving challenge that I am trying to meet. Next to this very pragmatic approach, ceramics is an amazing medium with which I love to play. I am still experimenting a lot, and it's a constant learning process,' she explains.

Reflecting on some of her biggest challenges, Lucile says that the joy is in knowing what she has achieved. She enjoys seeing her work stocked in different shops, and people contacting her to tell her how much they love her work.

Above: Lucile is best known for her blue-and-white works.

CLAY

'There is a lot of making and trying things out, plenty of unexpected results and, at the same time, observation. It's interesting to look back at your work and realize how organically it grew.'

Above: Each pattern Lucile creates on her signature blue-and-white wares is completely unique.
Opposite: Lucile's works are made from slip-cast porcelain and employ a limited range of colours.

Lynda Draper

Rather than concentrating on a particular technique or process, Lynda Draper uses clay as a material to communicate ideas and feelings, or to mediate loss and change. Her style, therefore, seems to evolve in response to her personal circumstances and experiences, as well as her vision. 'My work often explores psychological scenarios, at times representing a journey within the dualities of life and death, reality and fantasy, past and present,' she describes. 'I am interested in the relationship between the mind and material world and the related phenomenon of the metaphysical. Creating art is a way of attempting to bridge the gap between these different worlds.'

For a long time Lynda worked only with white porcelaneous stoneware, utilizing its ethereal qualities, but in recent times her practice has evolved quite dramatically due to her life's events. The recent reintroduction of colour has brought a sense of playfulness to the work, the pinched and coloured surfaces reminiscent of work she made more than twenty years earlier. 'This feels like a major breakthrough in the development of my practice and it is liberating to work in different ways, letting past practice inform some works. I am finding in my latest body of work a return to achromatic surfaces in an attempt to conjure ghostlike images with a dreamlike quality,' explains Lynda.

In the process of making, Lynda utilizes many different clays and glazes depending on her vision for a work, preferring to work in a way that leaves her options after the firing process and to allow any mishaps to inform the outcome. Multiple firings almost always occur, and she finds this provides an additional freedom in the creative process.

For Lynda, memories of childhood are slippery and elusive but many involve the pleasure and solace that came from making things, a joy that has continued throughout her life. 'I am fortunate enough to have been able to continuously make ceramic works, and also to be mentored by so many wonderful artists who work inside and outside the field of ceramics,' she says.

In 1980, directly out of high school, Lynda was accepted to study at what is currently UNSW Art and Design in Sydney, where she chose ceramics as a major as part of an arts education degree. Feeling the need to extend her technical skills and focus on a career in the field of ceramics, she went on to study at the National Art School – a disciplined and very intensive ceramics program – where she was mentored by Graham Oldroyd and Bill Samuels.

Left: Lynda's art is highly abstract, an attempt to bridge the gap between the mind and the material world.

Some two decades later, Lynda completed a Master of Fine Arts at UNSW Art and Design, thus rounding off a very formal and thorough arts education. 'I am very lucky to have experienced, and to have been part of, such an amazing educational environment: to have had the chance to study at institutions with such a rich tradition and legacy,' she says. Now Head of Ceramics at the National Art School in Sydney, Lynda will tell you that it is at this very institution that she learned the importance of transferring skills and knowledge, and the significance of mentorship, all of which have informed her career as an artist and an educator within the ceramics field.

Given the current resurgence of interest in ceramics, Lynda says it is exciting to see how many artists have branched out and begun to introduce ceramics into their art practice, bringing their different sensibilities and approaches to the material. 'While embracing the traditions of ceramic practice as an artist and an educator, I am motivated to foster a diverse contemporary dialogue between all aspects of arts practice.'

The recipient of many accolades, not least the Premier Acquisition Award at the 54th International Competition of Contemporary Ceramic Art, Lynda's reflections on her craft are philosophical. 'Follow your heart and trust your instincts, open your mind to endless possibilities. Learn from your mistakes and disappointments. Don't always expect success and acceptance of your work. Mentor and be generous to others. Regardless, keep making and when things are going wrong, play, take a risk, let go and the outcome may surprise you.'

Above and opposite: Lynda has recently reintroduced colour into her work, giving it renewed playfulness and vibrancy.

'There is always a part of the process that is out of your control, often giving rise to great expectations, wonder and sometimes disappointment.'

Above and opposite: Lynda varies the clays and glazes she uses according to her vision for the individual work.

Madeleine Preston

When Madeleine Preston went to art school, you either did fine art – painting, sculpture, photography, drawing or printmaking – or you did ceramics. Ceramics was in a separate school altogether and viewed by the painting department as 'craft'. The word craft – like the word decorative – was, for her generation of painters, a pejorative term. So Madeleine studied painting and practised as a painter for twenty years. She didn't start working with clay until May 2014, when she undertook a residency at TAFE in Sydney with Lynda Draper.

Now, with a practice in ceramics, Madeleine works primarily with coil hand building, although she is beginning to incorporate other techniques such as slab building. 'I have also started to throw – really badly – as I like the idea of combining shapes in a similar way to how Peter Voulkos did for a period of his career, but also in the precise way someone like Hans Coper did,' she explains.

Madeleine says her 'problem' has always been that she does not have one 'style', which makes it hard for dealers to sell work that is not presented as consistent. However, it's Madeleine's ideas that are the constant, not the way she represents them. 'I am interested in how the past informs the present and how it is used to justify behaviours and attitudes to aesthetics, politics and communities. I look at all sorts of images and forms, some from contemporary artists and a lot of images from pre-Christian Europe.'

Thinking back to the anecdotes shared by other resident artists she has worked with, Madeleine explains that the key material difference when working with clay is that it involves patience. Clay, it seems, is an endurance performance and ceramics is an equation of form over time. 'I feel overwhelmed when I hear people talk about spending years getting the right white, or a lifetime spent perfecting a pink glaze,' she says. 'I respect the importance of that knowledge and the knowledge that is embodied in different ceramicists, but I want to make and build in a different way, and am happy to use paint or room temperature glazing if needed to create the work I want to make.'

Madeleine found that when she started making vessels they functioned for her not as vases or storage containers but as people. The forms came with bodily analogies – 'neck', 'body' and 'feet' – but also with the weight of their own function. 'My works are not vases or even decorative vases, but like the Tanagra figurines they now contain meaning as objects and cyphers for history. It interests me that people find the vases beautiful, if not wonky,' she explains.

Left: Madeleine mainly employs hand-building techniques in her work.

For Madeleine, her forms are almost double agents, promising one thing but delivering another. They may be appealing due to their familiarity or apparent prosaic function, but Madeleine reads the vase form as a human figure. Conceptually she wants the pieces to challenge the history of bourgeois notions of 'good taste' and the forgotten or overlooked nature of function in art.

Madeleine prefers to work with larger ceramic installations that include other sculptural forms and painting, to create a place in which the pots can exist. The actual space for the work and the combination of medium serve to further the archival narrative.

As with many ceramicists, Madeleine concedes that important lessons are born of errors. She cites one occasion when she made a series of urns without keeping any record of the clay used to make them.

Not knowing at the time that you can have white earthenware, Madeleine assumed that they were all white clay and thus must all be stoneware. 'I particularly loved two of the urns and was very pleased with myself. The work was bisqued and it survived bisquing, but when it was glazed it melted. My hubris was lying in a pool on the kiln shelf,' Madeleine shares. 'To make things worse it took two or three other people's work with it. I was mortified. When I got some work documented I asked the photographer to shoot it as well as a permanent reminder. It's called *Overfired and Overtired*.'

Above: Madeleine wants her works to challenge ideas of good taste and preconceived notions about art.
Opposite: Showing the work of fellow ceramicist Shannon Duffy, which was subsumed by Madeleine's piece during the misfiring of her work.

Above and opposite: Madeleine's works are symbolic figurines rather than purely functional vessels.

'By presenting my works in a museum or archive context, I am able to point to fashions and dogmas in museology.'

Maria de Haan

Maria de Haan sees ceramics as a way to capture both a place and a moment in time. 'I want to understand clay, to know where it comes from and how it was made. I like to think about the person who made the piece, to imagine them making it'.

Like many other practising potters, Maria was initially exposed to clay through an evening class, while teaching English as a foreign language by day. She felt the hunger to supplement her life with something creative, having always loved creating as a child, and it took only one class on the wheel for her to know that her equilibrium had been altered forever. 'It all changed for me then as I developed this immense desire for knowledge. I quit my job and took every kind of course possible, and sought out every opportunity to learn as much as I could,' she explains.

Not content to stop there, Maria decided that she needed to be in a working ceramics environment, so completed an apprenticeship at a pottery in London, followed by a one-on-one course with renowned potter Simon Leach in Spain. A residency on a remote island in the West Indies was to follow, working alongside potter Mike Goddard over two winters. By 2008, Maria felt ready to establish her own studio in London and began to work at her ceramics practice full-time,

setting up a second studio in Deià, Mallorca, in 2015, where she now lives most of the year. She recommends that those starting out in ceramics follow a similar path. 'Do an apprenticeship or go and work for a while for a potter. You will learn so many valuable tips that you will carry with you throughout your career. Go to many ceramic fairs, talk to potters and ask around for opportunities, as often the best ones are not advertised. Learn to throw well, then develop your own style and go for it.'

Maria's practice is focused on making sculptural vessels and minimalist tableware. 'My early pieces, when I was making tableware, were deeply influenced by the Japanese aesthetic. Now that I am making more sculptural pieces I am generally attracted to the natural minimal aesthetic of the wabi-sabi style. I travel a lot and I gather inspiration from natural forms, stone textures and rocks. I spend a lot of time in the sea, strangely, and I am hugely inspired by underwater coral forms,' she reveals. It was indeed some coral formations off the coast of a small French Antilles archipelago that formed the inspirational basis of her now-signature vessel forms. 'These formations were large and very beautiful, slightly closed in form and in a dark aubergine colour with an amazing rock-like

Left: Maria in her studio,
surrounded by her works.

texture. They were very mysterious, and I have never seen anything like them since.'

All Maria's pots are wheel thrown and her most recent work is smoke-fired porcelain. She fires the pots in metal barrels, using wood and sawdust and natural materials such as salt, fruits and vegetable skins. The pots are all unique as it is the fire that controls the outcome, and each piece has its own journey into fire.

Maria is most proud of her smoke-fired work. 'I was inspired after randomly reading a book on it as a firing method and I decided to try it for myself. It was the process that inspired me, and not anyone else's work, which is interesting as it has always been the other way around,' she says. 'I went in completely blind with an open mind and no expectations for the outcome. It was a pure experiment. I had no idea that I would fall

in love with smoke firing and it would become the main method I use.'

Maria's other work is fired in an electric kiln, using a heavily grogged clay. 'The more grog the better. I like to leave areas of the pot unglazed so you just have the natural, raw beauty of the clay itself, which focuses the attention to the form and texture of the piece,' she explains.

While Maria does concede that an occupation in ceramics is very physically demanding, with long hours, for her this effort is more than validated when someone buys a really special piece and they love it just as much as she does.

Above and opposite: Most of Maria's recent work is smoke fired in metal barrels.

'I absolutely love smoke firing. The idea that you can use fire to decorate a pot is absolutely fascinating to me.'

Maryam Riazi

Working with clay has always been very therapeutic for Maryam Riazi. When she starts making something, a story starts to form in her thoughts, usually involving people she knows, nature or animals. 'These stories and thoughts have given my pieces a certain personality and character, which I think has become my signature, these reflections of what I imagine.'

Discovering her love for ceramics later on in life, Maryam had gone through different careers, none ever quite bringing her a sense of fulfilment. She took a ceramics class for fun a few years back, and has not stopped making since. 'I think playing with clay as a child helped me build an emotional relationship with it. Working with clay now brings me a sense of peacefulness and comfort, which I have not experienced in anything else,' she explains.

Maryam grew up in Shiraz, a city in southern Iran known for its poets, crafts and beautiful historical architecture, and she feels she is very fortunate to have had that exposure growing up. 'I lived in a community full of other children, ancient sycamore trees and open fields. I spent a lot of time outside being surrounded and perhaps inspired by nature. I think that connection has influenced my work more than anything else.'

It is the process of forming the clay and feeling its texture that Maria finds most enjoyable. 'I find it fascinating to see something as mundane as clay transform into new objects and forms. Working with clay engages my creative mind. It gives me the same feeling as hiking a mountain or feeling the morning breeze,' she describes.

Until recently Maryam mostly used Black Mountain Clay, a dark, chocolate-coloured clay, which she loves for its earthiness and texture. Her pieces are high-fired at cone 10, which makes them much denser and stronger. More recently she has started working with lighter-coloured clays, giving her newer works a lighter, more colourful glaze.

Aside from the joy of working with clay, what Maryam enjoys most are the behind-the-scenes aspects of pottery. 'You meet so many amazing potters who share your core and passion. I am yet to meet a potter I didn't like! The community is loving, warm and passionate.' It is the marketing of her work that she finds confronting and uncomfortable. 'I started doing pottery as a hobby and, like most artists, I don't enjoy the selling of my work,' she admits. 'But I quickly started to feel awkward about making more work unless I found homes for what I'd already made.

Left: Maryam loves the
earthiness and texture
of Black Mountain Clay.

Although social media has made marketing my work
a more pleasant experience, I still find the practice of
selling less than desirable.'

Maryam left her home in Shiraz a year after the
Iran–Iraq war started, changing her life forever. She
moved to the United States thinking it would be her
temporary home, and yet thirty-five years on she still
lives in Los Angeles and has grown to love the city for
its melting pot of cultural differences. 'I love what I do
and have surrounded myself with people and things
that bring me joy. I'm very fortunate to be able to
donate a major portion of my sales to animal charities.
Making these small differences are undoubtedly my
proudest moments.'

Above and opposite: Maryam has recently experimenting with lighter-coloured clays, which allow her to make brighter, more colourful pieces.

'I love the versatility of clay. It can be sculptural and presented in an art gallery, or functional, as a tool in our daily lives.'

Milly Dent

Above: Milly has quickly established herself on the ceramics scene.

Milly Dent's evolution from student to popular ceramics brand has been swift. Having always harboured a desire to make, she moved from Brisbane to Sydney to study a Bachelor of Design at the College of Fine Arts (now UNSW Art and Design). 'I started working with clay and everything fell into place. Using the material was intriguing and exciting and I enjoyed exploring all the possibilities, as well as discovering the limitations,' she reflects.

Graduating in 2013, Milly followed went on to further study in Montreal for six months. During this time she gained a true appreciation for the capacity of clay and expanded her style with this new and different perspective on making. 'I returned to Sydney and I knew I wanted to keep making. I started making for friends, then friends of friends, until the time came that I needed to set up my own small studio space and buy my own kiln.'

Milly's design style and philosophy are based on the notion of putting practical, unique and thoughtful pieces of handmade design into the world. Her style plays on traditional blue and white porcelain wares, and warps this to create contemporary pieces that are frozen in the fluid motion used to create them. She aims for a clean and balanced style through the inclusion of geometric facets and fluid marbling patterns. 'My creative process is very intuitive and unpredictable as it employs a mix of techniques. These include marbling clay and slip-casting techniques to create unique colours and patterns in contemporary, fine and translucent forms. The process of making gives me the biggest satisfaction in my work and I intend my pieces to be a mixture of both sculpture and function.'

The two biggest influences on Milly's work are the ceramic itself, as well as the sea. As part of her process, she takes photographs of objects, shapes and the ocean, prior to initial sketching and mood boarding to find forms, colours and textures. Natural elements are reflected in her work, with colours and patterns related to the ocean prevalent throughout her range of work.

Milly works with Australian porcelain, cobalt stains and clear gloss glazes, using moulds that are made of existing forms or forms

that she has carved from plaster. The marbling–casting part of
the process is very intuitive and fluid, and allows Milly to push the
boundaries even if it means a lot of disasters before one success. 'It
makes the success all the more rewarding!' she says. 'Luckily I enjoy
almost every stage of my process, but I get enormous satisfaction
from opening up the glaze kiln after the final firing and seeing the
results of the previous week's work. It is only at this point you can see
the vitrified and translucent qualities as well as the true colours of
the porcelain,' she says.

Milly's rapid establishment in the Australian ceramics scene has
been an exercise in harnessing opportunities. Through combining a
strong and recognizable aesthetic, a clear vision for her brand, and
the powers of social media, Milly has garnered a strong and loyal
following. Her work is now sold through a vast network and has been
included in several gallery exhibitions.

Above: The patterns of the sea
are a significant influence on
Milly's work.

'The possibility to create something that you can fire to a vitreous permanent state that will stand the test of time is a great motivator.'

Above: Milly mixes slip using a drill fitted with a paint mixing attachment before sieving the clay for mould pouring.
Opposite: Milly's pieces are a contemporary take on traditional blue-and-white porcelain ware.

Mizuyo Yamashita

There was a single piece of work that led Mizuyo Yamashita to work with clay: a pot by internationally renowned artist Grayson Perry in the exhibition *I Am a Camera* at the Saatchi Gallery in London. For Mizuyo, a vase was simply something beautiful to hold flowers or to be displayed in a tokonoma (a recess, just above floor level, for displaying flowers and ornaments in a Japanese house). 'But Grayson's pot was full of strong messages – and some ugly images – and he completely changed this idea for me and made me want to know more about pottery,' she explains.

After seeing Grayson Perry's work Mizuyo enrolled in a local adult-education college 'just to see'. She spent two days per week experimenting with papers, basketry materials and clay, as well as working as an assistant for a ceramicist who was making tableware with a jigger jolley machine. Fortuitously one of the teachers in the college invited Mizuyo to join his Christmas craft fair, and after receiving unexpectedly positive feedback and making contacts, she started selling her small porcelain bowls to shops. 'I don't feel like I chose this path, but I followed my interest, as there [is] so much mystery in ceramics and I wanted to know more about it and get better at it,' she explains.

Through further work and study, Mizuyo continued exploring the possibilities in ceramics, and realized that what she most enjoyed was making small things, with her graduate-show work being an installation consisting of small objects.

Mizuyo explains that the reason for basing her work on 'standard' shapes, rather than relying entirely on her own aesthetics, is because she is a Japanese maker creating for a European audience. 'Something that has become standard must be loved, but I don't always feel the same way. They might like a certain object for aesthetic value but I might like it for exoticism or novelty, either Japanizing the shapes that are popular, or Europeanizing the shapes familiar to me. My work falls somewhere between the two.'

Mizuyo's work often uses neutral tones. Sometimes she introduces colour to provide an accent to the design of an individual piece, or to add effect within a group of pieces. 'I use a variety of clay – terracotta; white, grogged, speckled and black stoneware clay; and porcelain. I mix them depending on the design simply to get the right colour and texture, to achieve a certain effect in combination with the glaze or just to enjoy the random result. I also mix stones and glaze into the clay to change the quality of it or to get some effect in the surface.'

After throwing, Mizuyo treats the surface of her work with decorating techniques such as shinogi

Left: Mizuyo most enjoys making works on a smaller scale.

(fluting), mentori (faceting), and zogan (inlaying). She has also become familiar with the process of kintsugi, a Japanese repairing technique that uses lacquer and gold. 'I repair my own work as well as others.' Sometimes it creates beautiful character to the piece, highlighting the heartbreaking moment when you broke it. It can cost more than the pot itself to repair this way but I appreciate the fact somebody is appreciating so much of our work,' she admits.

Mizuyo finds it difficult to articulate what ceramics means to her personally, but suspects the appeal might be that clay acts like a mirror. 'It makes me see myself more objectively. The more I do it, the more I find what I like, what I value and what is changing.'

Mizuyo also has many family memories associated with ceramics, most obviously her family get-togethers around the dinner table. Her grandmother owned a ceramics shop selling everyday pieces, and Mizuyo loved to visit, while her mother always taught her the importance of various items in the cooking and serving process, selecting from their collection of hundreds of handmade pieces.

Most fondly, Mizuyo recalls a potter friend of her father's who used to make pottery for tea ceremonies. 'He would bring a lump of clay for us to make something to go into his anagama kiln. I would make small pinched and coiled bowls and visit him during his five-day firings,' she says. 'I live such a different life from my family now, but by doing ceramics I feel I'm connected with them, talking with those whom I can no longer see but who made me who I am now.'

Above: Mizuyo's pieces often make use of neutral tones.
Opposite: Mizuyo at work on her studio.

'The main purpose of my ceramics is to make beautiful objects to be looked at, touched and used ... I make everyday objects that fit in simple homes.'

CLAY

Above: Mizuyo's tools and examples of her ceramics range laid out in her studio.
Opposite: After throwing, Mizuyo treats the surface with decorating techniques such as shinogi.

Rachel Boxnboim

Rachel Boxnboim's relationship with ceramics started at the age of seven, when her family was living next door to a ceramic artist who gave lessons to the local children. Later on, while attending art school, she chose to major in industrial design, even though ceramics was always her first passion. 'When I started working on my final project the process led me back to ceramics – this time in the slip version of it – and I fell in love all over again,' she says.

This project – her final work at the industrial design department at Bezalel Academy of Arts and Design in Jerusalem – was named *Alice*. Beginning with just a teapot, Rachel cast an entire ceramic tea service, including cups, plates, a sugar container and a milk jug, inside fabric moulds by pouring liquid clay into stitched cloth and gradually syringing it out again, leaving a thick layer clinging to the inside of the mould. The cloth burned away when fired, leaving the delicate ceramic vessels behind, mimicking the fabric's behaviour without it being there.

In that project, Rachel made the connection between fabric and ceramic – between soft and hard – a connection that continues to inform her work. The ceramic takes on the texture of the fabric and the appearance of the seams, yet in a hardened form. Rachel tries out different patterns and fabrics, with the form of the utensil being determined by the pattern – or at least, considerably influenced by it. The pieces are indeed useful, yet all contain an element of whimsy and surprise. 'The sets are functional, however

... the fabric burns off with each firing so no mould can be used twice – it is a very labour-intensive way to create,' Rachel notes. The shapes are also difficult to machine sew, so producing the pieces on a mass scale would be very difficult. For Rachel, the time spent on each piece is part of her work's charm. 'It's part of my philosophy – the story of me sitting down and sewing each item, using fabrics I've hand-picked and that I love,' she says.

Rachel grew up in a design-oriented family, with parents who were design buyers and diligent about taking their children to museums and galleries. 'I believe growing up like this teaches you to pay attention to details and truly care about what items around you look like,' says Rachel. 'Sometimes it is so difficult and you ask yourself "Why couldn't I go to law school or something?" but at the end of the day, we spent our days with this amazing material, surrounded by beauty and creation.'

A few months after Rachel graduated from Bezalel, a major design company approached her, wanting to purchase her ceramic designs. Rachel was flattered and excited by the proposal, and started working vigorously on the task – her first large order and also the first time she produced items for sale. 'My technique wasn't developed enough. When opening the first kiln – it turned out that I hadn't solved all the technical issues and every item had a crack on the bottom. I was devastated! I have since learned from this mistake,' she says.

Left: Rachel's works get their fluid quality from her making process, which involves pouring liquid clay into cloth and then syringing it out.

'My work is all about the texture. I am obsessed with fabrics and whenever I see a nice texture in a garment or home textile – I'll purchase it in order to cast in it!'

CLAY

Above and opposite: There is a connection between hard ceramic and soft fabric in Rachel's work, as the ceramic pieces take on the texture of the fabric used to mould them.

Ruby Pilven

Ruby Pilven thinks it's a great time to be a ceramic artist. 'We are amidst a craft revolution – a movement where society is slowly appreciating the art of the handmade again,' she says. Ruby knows firsthand people's mounting desire to learn how ceramics are made, to touch them, appreciate them, and to admire the craftspeople who make them.

Having grown up with ceramicist parents (Janine and Peter Pilven), Ruby has always been surrounded by ceramics in some way, whether it was playing in the studio, watching her parents making pots, attending exhibitions or visiting fellow potter friends. 'I've had a passion and fascination for clay my entire life, but it wasn't until I was doing my studio art folio in my final year of high school that I realized how strong this interest was,' she admits.

Her pottery peerage coupled with her passion seemed to indicate that she was destined to work with clay, but, rather surprisingly, her parents spent years trying to usher Ruby away from a career in art. She reached a compromise by completing a double degree at Monash University in visual arts and business. It was there that Ruby strengthened her drawing and print skills, and learned how to successfully market herself via platforms such as Instagram. Even as a student, she would make rings and brooches in her spare time and earn a modest income by selling these to small regional galleries.

Once she completed her degree, Ruby participated in some group exhibitions and focused on exploring different methods of making her work. It was during this time that her new colourful jewellery and homewares range was born, and interest in her work has grown so steadily that Ruby is now in the fortunate position of working full-time in the studio.

With no formal training in ceramics, Ruby has gathered skills from both parents and gained knowledge from attending exhibitions, speaking to friends, reading books and watching YouTube videos. Her style of work is audacious in its bold colour patterns, striking in its gold lustre highlights and distinctive in its simplicity of form. Employing a contemporary twist on the Japanese technique of nerikomi, Ruby uses stoneware and porcelain clays, which she colours with specific stains.

There are numerous stages involved in Ruby's work so she is, at various times, creating fresh works, glazing, decorating or firing the kiln. Creating her ceramics always begins with wedging the coloured clay bodies, then flattening them out on a slab roller, creating a poetic colourful dance over the top, and then sculpting them into a particular form.

Left: Ruby keeps her forms simple but uses bold colour and patterns.

'The layered patterns in my work are a mixture of controlled and spontaneous movements, giving my work an element of unpredictability that allows it to be recognizable yet unique each time. Revealing the final pattern has an element of surprise every time.'

In her wheel-thrown works, Ruby has been exploring a contemporary twist on traditional Japanese tea bowls and beakers, using thumbholes, foot rings and loose but functional forms.

The distinctive nature of Ruby's work draws on multiple contemporary influences, such as music, design and culture. 'I'm heavily influenced by my mother's use of colour in her 2D and 3D works; my father's lustre work in the 1980s and his organic throwing sensibility; the Japanese ceramic technique of nerikomi; the overuse of gold in ancient civilizations; artists such as Miró, Matisse and Pollock; Middle Eastern fabric patterns; and everyday living experiences such as the natural swells of the beach tide, the natural colourants from fruits, and the flocking of birds in the sky,' she explains.

Ruby also enjoys the social aspect of ceramics. 'For me it's not just the learning and making, but the sharing nature of ceramics that makes it so beautiful. This sense of belonging and collective knowledge is priceless and it's why the community is so supportive.'

One of Ruby's proudest achievements is her collaboration with the National Gallery of Victoria design store in connection with the gallery's exhibition *Masterpieces from the Hermitage: The legacy of Catherine the Great*. She made a collection influenced by the exhibition, to be sold and distributed throughout the NGV design stores.

Above: Ruby's ceramic jewellery is decorated with gold lustre.
Opposite: Ruby at work in her studio.

'Ceramics is my life. It not only represents a way of seeing and living in daily life for me but it also holds an important part in my family heritage, a sense of belonging.'

Above and opposite: Ruby's coloured clay bodies are first wedged, then flattened out on a slab roller before they are sculpted into forms.

Sean Gerstley

Above: Sean's *Little Lemon Vase*.

When Sean Gerstley enrolled in the Rhode Island School of Design, he opted to major in ceramics, despite never having worked with clay. 'I think I just wanted a totally new tool in my bag,' he says. That was eight years ago, and he has been a practising ceramicist since.

Notions of style are not something that Sean is especially concerned with in his practice, but he describes his work as lingering in a zone that's 'both primitive and futuristic'. Clay has a significant meaning to him, when he considers it in the context of the vast history of the medium. 'Almost every culture on the planet has manipulated and fired clay in some way for millennia. So ceramics represents humanity in lots of ways. How do we eat? What do we value?' Sean reflects.

Creatively, Sean looks to the likes of sculptors Ron Nagle and Matt Wedel, artists Viola Frey and Arlene Shechet, and ceramicists Anders Ruhwald, Betty Woodman, Linda Sormin and Beatrice Wood as sources of inspiration for his work. He also refers to the Chicago Imagists and to contemporary furniture as being among his very diverse influences.

What Sean loves is that his primary tools are his hands. What he likes less, however, is glaze. 'Glaze is a constant pain in the neck. I want an intern to do glaze testing all day for me because I don't have the patience to measure out all the toxic powders,' he admits.

He uses all kinds of clay, but right now Sean is focused on using a body that's half porcelain and half terracotta, and he almost exclusively works using a hand-built technique. 'Most of the work is made by pinching together stacks of coils that have been squashed flat, creating my signature manic pinched texture,' he describes.

Sean suggests the best way to master clay is by making as much as possible. 'Sometimes we just have to work through enough things to figure out what we really should be making.'

As to whether the current interest in ceramics is merely transient, Sean's thoughts are wry. 'I think it's funny when people tell me that clay is in right now or it's breaking out and becoming trendy. It's funny, because I've been hearing that for years. Ceramics has always been something we love, right? Like for 26,000 years? Maybe as technology dominates the attention of our hands and eyes and minds in our daily lives, we look at the handmade with more lust than we used to.'

Above: Sean's technique of pinching together stacks of coils creates his signature 'manic' texture.

CLAY

'I'm influenced
as much by
gardening, cooking,
honky-tonk music,
American divas,
conspiracy theories,
and hydrotherapy
as I am by other
creatives.'

Above and opposite: Sean describes his work as 'both primitive and futuristic'.

Sophie Harle

Despite having her interest in ceramics ignited in high school, and obtaining a Bachelor of Fine Arts majoring in ceramics at university, Australian Sophie Harle ultimately thought it was 'unreasonable' to actually expect a career in clay. Instead she worked for a decade in decidedly non-ceramicist roles in PR and market research, relegating the making of pots to her spare time. 'I did so many short courses that they became long courses,' she says.

Then five years ago a change of circumstances presented the opportunity to realize her dream to start potting full-time. 'I grabbed it with both hands and haven't looked back. I've officially been practising full-time for a handful of years, but I've been making pots whenever I can for about twenty!' says Sophie.

Espousing the qualities of simplicity and minimalism, Sophie's aesthetic is very pared back and honest. She prefers quiet and contemplative pots that serve their function and don't compete for attention. Her palette is mostly made up of neutral, earthy tones and she likes to experiment with different clays. 'I mix a lot of my own clay, using found clay and recycled throwing scraps, so there's a very organic, gutsy quality to my clay body. I love subtle variations in surface and finish. I'm all about subtlety,' she says.

Sophie views her work with ceramics as being about connection: to history, to nature, to life, and a link through time and between people. Her daily morning walks are instrumental in channelling this connectedness, allowing her important thinking time.

'That time of quiet contemplation helps me organize my ideas. It settles me, and my pots come out of that quiet place of introspection,' she explains.

What Sophie loves is the sense that clay as her medium is alive, and that vitality manifests itself as unpredictability and tactility. Sophie is constantly motivated to try new things, always experimenting with variations on shapes – a new type of handle, different clays, new glaze recipes – with much of her inspiration born of her fluid making process itself. Her favourite Australian potters are Prue Venables and Phil Elson, as she resonates with their ceaseless experimentation and enthusiasm for pushing materials to the limit.

One of Sophie's biggest delights is knowing that people use her pieces. 'I love it when people share that they eat breakfast out of one of my bowls each morning, as in a funny way a little part of me is sharing that with them,' she says. 'My bowl or plate or cup is part of their life and they get pleasure from the experience of using it. It's so gratifying to be part of that exchange.'

Having traversed the path to a full-time ceramics practice the long way, Sophie is probably well qualified to dispense some advice to others about what is important on such a journey. 'Find a mentor – find people who are better at making pots than you – and talk to them, and spend time at their studios. Be a sponge, listen and be excited about learning all the time,' she suggests. 'Pottery is a constant challenge so embracing that challenge will make you happy.'

Left: Sophie in her
Brunswick studio.

'My techniques are very traditional. I'm not into flashy effects. I like my pots to be honest, to retain some of the energy of the making.'

Above: Sophie mixes her own clay and values the organic quality that this brings to her work.
Opposite and following pages: Sophie uses a limited, neutral palette, letting the beauty of her work reside in its simplicity.

Sophie Moran

Sophie Moran loves simple, functional forms with surface treatments that reflect a timeless aesthetic. As a maker of ceramics for nearly twenty years, she describes her overall aim as creating vessels that return significance and meaning to an everyday household object. She also hopes that they can be handled, utilized and enjoyed on a daily basis – and hopefully for a very long time.

After completing secondary school, Sophie undertook a Bachelor of Arts majoring in philosophy and literature, though it took her a number of years, post study, to find out what it was that she wanted to commit to professionally. 'I tried further studies in anthropology and work in overseas aid, but as a fairly introverted soul I found the best way I could connect with others was through the handmade object.'

Sophie completed a couple of courses in wheel-thrown pottery, followed by a Diploma of Art (Ceramics). She finished her studies in 1998 and has been a full-time professional potter since.

Sophie aims for honest expression in her work, which reflects her character. Her collections range from ornamental, statement pieces to quiet utilitarian forms. As Sophie says, 'This diversity allows me to express different elements of my personality'.

Using both porcelain and stoneware clay, Sophie starts all her work on the potter's wheel, where she merges traditional and modern throwing techniques. Sometimes she will apply oxides, stains and under-glazes for decorative mark making, and she has developed a library of glazes that often have a matte or satin finish. Sophie then fires her works in an electric kiln to 1280°C. 'I hand form, decorate, glaze and fire every piece myself. I have a macabre enjoyment of the labour-intensive process as it concentrates my awareness of the fine details, encouraging a slower pace and an appreciation of the importance of every step. It is this intention and care in making that makes each piece special.'

Born and bred in Melbourne, Sophie sees herself as a product of her environment. The impact of her locality on her work is also very significant, as she develops new ideas through keen observation of the people and places around her. 'I love both urban and rural settings and am drawn to marks and patterns that reflect my surroundings,' Sophie says. 'As a maker of functional tableware I am also interested in how meals are served in the homes of my community. I am fortunate to live in a multicultural society where the diversity in home-cooked food is boundless.'

Left: Sophie at work on the potter's wheel, where all her pieces begin.

Her favourite parts of the making process are the throwing and turning stages of creating a pot. While she enjoys the intellectual challenge in glaze development, surface treatments and firing, the intuitive nature of form creation is what draws her back to the studio day after day. 'My understanding of the science behind glaze development is fairly basic, so I find resolving issues that occur during glaze-firing quite challenging. But it is a challenge that I enjoy. One of the hardest things is finding the time to trial and test new work while meeting orders for existing work,' she says. 'As a teacher of ceramics I encourage repetition and intention in making as I feel this is the best way to refine the skills needed for this craft. It is important to let go of things that aren't working and be aware that whatever is fired will be around for a very, very long time!'

Like many current ceramicists, Sophie looks to 20th-century potter Lucie Rie as her muse, appreciating her independence of approach and style when so many around her were toeing the popular line. 'I love Lucie's ability to create timeless, quiet, unassuming pieces that are lauded globally today. Her pots make me cry, in a good way!' she admits.

CLAY

Above: Over twenty years, Sophie has developed a library of glazes to use in her work.
Opposite: Sophie's pieces are designed to be used every day in the home.

Steen Ipsen

Above: Steen surrounded by his works.

Having practised ceramics for 25 years, Steen Ipsen warns that to have a career in clay you must be fully cognisant that you will surrender your whole life to it. 'You will never have as much spare time as other people. I think, however, that no one can achieve greater happiness than clay makers. You simply have to love it, and be completely absorbed by working with this medium. When I notice that students and trainees have the right understanding of the material I encourage them to continue working with clay,' he explains. 'If you don't have the right attitude, then my advice is that you look for another education.'

When Steen was young, he says he was always more creative than he was academically talented. Having recognized early that he was fundamentally and enduringly impressed by the possibilities that clay presented, he studied the craft, ultimately becoming head of the Institute of Glass and Ceramics at the Royal Danish Academy of Fine Arts, School of Design from 1996 to 2004. Now living and working in Copenhagen, Steen is considered one of the most influential ceramicists of his generation, demonstrating a profound knowledge of materials and technique.

Steen's style is simple, with a powerful graphical appearance. Some of the pieces consist of joined, simply-coloured spherical elements that are subsequently tied with coloured strings and ropes of PVC and leather. Others explore materials in an organic pattern of broken or continuous connecting lines. The result is an abstract and highly spatial sculptural expression. Ipsen has a fascination – perhaps even obsession – with the spherical shape.

Form and decoration are both central to Steen's work and are often closely integrated. 'My objects could also be made from other materials but ceramics is central in my works. In my hand-modelled sculptures you will often see decorative pattern where I seek to express the shapes more clearly and underline the movements in the objects,' explains Steen. 'In recent years I have worked with the sculptural ball element tied up in coloured strings in a line pattern, resulting in a highly spatial sculptural expression.'

Above: Steen's works are highly sculptural, often combining ceramic elements with other materials.

In Steen's pieces you can observe a close relationship with Scandinavian architecture, craft and design, which are among his inspirations. The objects are unique and made of earthenware. His process is sometimes based on clay elements modelled in shapes and then built up in terms and variations, and sometimes it is based on free hand-modelled objects. The shape is grown step-by-step and Steen gives himself time to reflect and change direction, setting his own rules as to where he seeks to obtain the relationship between the simple and the complex.

In Steen's organic hand-modelled works, he focuses on the shapes and contrasts of surfaces, the light and shadow of – and between – spaces. 'What interests me is precisely the impact obtained through a non-correct rendering of the geometric forms. Reflections of the glazes and the rhythmic displacement of the single elements in the sculptures are used freely for interpretations of the cubic abstraction, and for exploring multiple dimensions.'

CLAY

Above and opposite: Steen's works integrate decoration and form, with patterns highlighting the underlying shape.

Stine Dulong

When asked to describe how she feels about her work, Stine Dulong turns to a quote she once stumbled across by the German philosopher Immanuel Kant that said 'the hand is the window to the mind'. The quote stayed with her and she feels it conveys her relationship with clay.

After working in London as a business crime lawyer for several years, Stine never quite felt fulfilled or happy. She often felt like she went into work every day to perform a role that was written for someone else. She decided to do various evening courses, one of which was pottery. 'My teacher said that as soon as I touched the clay, she saw a look in my eyes that reminded her of when she was young and the instant love she had felt for the material. She was right. I knew instinctively that I had found where I was meant to be in life. I can't really explain it, other than there was simply no going back from that point onwards,' she says. Three years on, Stine is a full-time ceramicist, a profession she describes as a more 'present path'. 'For me, the making process – trying, failing and trying again – gives me an understanding and fulfilment that I never experienced before,' she explains.

Almost entirely self-taught, Stine recently enrolled in a two-year part-time diploma course in ceramic design in London to ensure that she becomes the maker she is meant to be, rather than the maker she has become through self-learning. Although at first most of her pieces were hand built, she is increasingly falling in love with the potter's wheel. 'Having always loved the use by Scandinavian artists and designers of natural materials such as leather, wood, stone, metal and clay, it's probably no surprise that I make most of my work with stoneware clay bodies,' she says. 'I can't think of anything more aesthetically pleasing than the mix of raw materials and sharp, light, airy designs.'

Stine describes how she sometimes lets the clay dictate what it wants to be – particularly on the wheel – which can prove to be a challenge when working on a specific order or project. 'I think that it's important, as a functional maker, to allow these creative moments to take over once in a while. Otherwise, you end up making the same thing over and over and the joy gets lost somehow.'

Stine's brand, SkandiHus, is focused on handmade, high quality ceramics that are affordable, stylish and relevant to how people live. She tends to work with light colours inspired by her childhood in Denmark and seeks the understated impact of beautiful utilitarian Scandinavian design. Her biggest influence is not a

Left: Stine's tendency towards light colours is inspired by her childhood in Denmark.

ceramicist but rather the stripped-down buildings of early 20th-century Austrian architect Adolf Loos. Loos advocated for clearing the world of unnecessary ornaments to 'show the way' for the modern human being. He was not against good craftsmanship but argued that craftsmen were forced to waste their time on ornamentation that meant the object would become obsolete more quickly. 'For him, the distinction was not between complicated and simple designs but rather between "organic" and "superfluous" decorations,' Stine explains. 'I try to adhere to these principles in my work, as I believe that quality design should be affordable, stylish and relevant to the modern human being by providing minimal distraction and maximum functionality and beauty.'

Admitting that she is often attracted to ceramic designs that are markedly different from her own,

Stine has considered one day moving away from minimalist design and trying out bold colours and patterns. 'But I've had to accept that what I make is really closely connected to my mind, heart and background and, as the years have gone by, I've come to rest with my designs and feel more at one with them,' she says.

Stine says the biggest challenge of her practice is striking a balance between making a living and keeping her products affordable – part of the bigger challenge of running a business and having time to be a maker. 'My advice to anyone wanting to follow in my footsteps would be to not forget the business side of things. Money seems to still be such a taboo for artists, but it's really important to have open and frank discussions about it. If you don't make a living from your art, you won't be able to continue making it.'

Above and opposite: Stine at work in her London studio.

Susan Robey

It was a chance brush with a travelling exhibition of UK ceramic artist Alison Britton's works while Susan Robey was an architecture student at the University of Sydney that first piqued her interest in clay. 'Her strong hand-built work was completely different from any ceramic art I had seen previously. I was smitten,' she recalls. 'I then took classes in ceramics as part of my architecture degree and was fortunate to be inspired and instructed by ceramic artists Patsy Healy and Susan Ostling. I later followed up with a degree in fine arts in Melbourne, and I've now been a practising ceramic artist for more than 20 years. I have great respect for the history of ceramics and its variety of cultural forms. I enjoy practising an ancient craft in a contemporary world and feeling part of this story. Ceramics to me represents beauty and endurance.'

As an architect and a ceramicist, it would be impossible for Susan to not be inspired by the built environment. 'I transform clay, the most humble of building materials, into hand-built ceramic objects that examine many aspects of architectural space. I consider concepts such as outside or inside, solid or hollow, open or enclosed,' she explains. Susan delights in details, such as the exploration of boundaries and edges and the study of mass and scale in form and surface texture. Her objects are closed, the interiors dark and mysterious, glimpsed briefly through piercings (or windows) in the enveloping boundary walls.

Susan selects and combines architectural elements – walls, columns, roofs – in unexpected ways. 'I create the illusion of movement, a hint of personality and the possibility of communication. Rising on columns or legs, the objects run and dance in defiance of gravity and their architectural underpinnings,' she describes.

It can take Susan several days to construct one work, which means it can be heartbreaking when a work she has grown quite fond of finally stands up for a moment, and then collapses under its own weight. 'This is because I have wrongly estimated the leg strength and have not listened to the material. Clay can be very unforgiving,' she admits. 'I try not to become too attached to a work too early in the process. Working at the limits can mean many failures before success.'

Susan is proud that she has transformed her architectural knowledge and experience into a unique approach to ceramics. Her technique is certainly challenging and requires perseverance – like the

Left: Susan draws on many elements of her architectural practice in her ceramics work. Here she creates a design for a new piece.

medium itself. 'Making my objects involves reimagining many techniques borrowed from architectural practice. I work with models to explore ideas. I use scaffolds to support my work at the plastic stage. I form joints using the mitres, scarfs and dowels of a carpenter. I am not a traditional maker,' she explains.

Susan works with liquid paper-clay slips to cast wafer-thin slabs from which she hand builds thin-walled, finely detailed ceramic objects with the lightness and fragility of crushed paper but the strength and solidity of buildings. Paper clay is a mixture of clay and a small amount of paper fibre that provides additional strength and flexibility. These qualities allow Susan to work with extremely thin material, with the paper fibre burning away in the firing process.

Susan explains that working with clay is a very tactile experience, involving the engagement of several senses simultaneously and a very direct hand–eye connection. 'There is always more to learn, which is why it is so appealing. It is an opportunity to embrace chance. Working with clay often requires spontaneous decisions,' she says. 'Clay can surprise you and appearances can be deceptive. I enjoy the challenge of combining creative ideas with the application of technical skills and knowledge – very similar to architectural practice but with total creative freedom. Working with clay is totally absorbing – it can make time stand still.'

Above and opposite: Susan is inspired by the built environment and her work has
a strong architectural feel.

'My approach brings
together my understanding
of architectural structure
and form, and the expressive
potential of clay pushed to its
technical limits.'

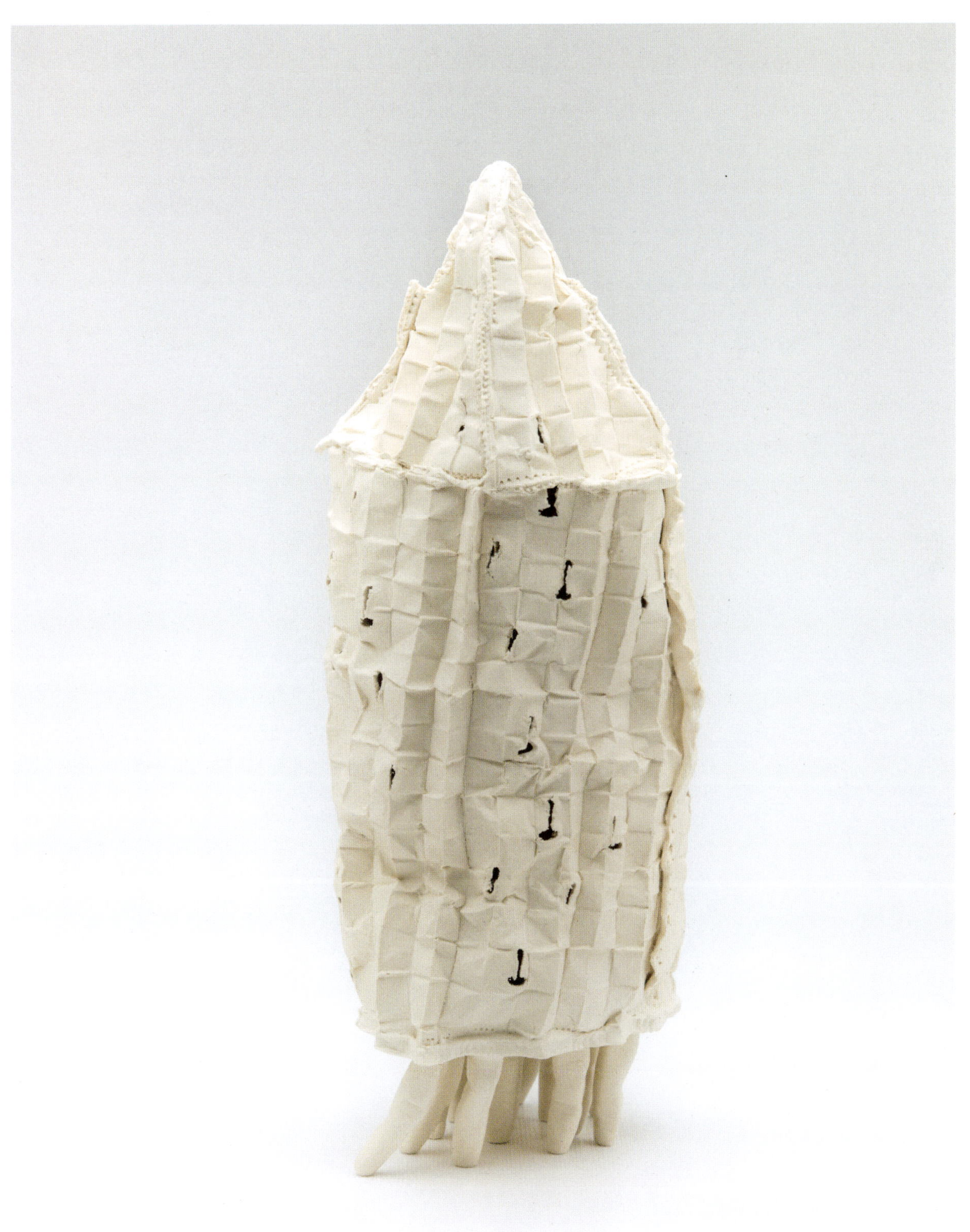

Tania Rollond

Tania Rollond confides that working with ceramics builds a certain grim fatalism, where the expectation of disaster is the norm. 'So the feeling of excitement and satisfaction when you're holding a good piece in your hands is pretty damn special!' she says.

Referencing artist and theorist Paul Mathieu, who wrote that ceramic objects are humanity's archive, Tania sees ceramics as 'a chance for me to add my own speck-of-dust-sized voice to this grand narrative, and a way to think about time,' she says. 'For almost as long as we humans have walked the Earth we have scratched or printed our individual marks and traces into the malleable, receptive surface of clay, and we have formed it into objects that play intimate roles in daily life.'

Mostly, Tania's work is wheel-thrown Southern Ice porcelain, with decorative elements that she draws using ceramic pencils or paints with ceramic stains and oxides. She also uses dark stoneware clay bodies, slips and inlaid line work, and loves to hand build, especially sculptural work, so there is always a range of activities afoot in her studio.

Straight out of high school Tania completed a degree in graphic design, but as soon as she hit the work force she knew it wasn't for her. After a period of uncertain, early-20s wandering she started several part-time art courses at technical college, and after taking just a few Saturday pottery classes she found herself completely addicted. 'I had never liked clay at school as it was too messy and uncontrollable, but encountering it later, I found this 'mind-of-its-own' quality to be a good challenge to my control-freak neatness,' she admits. 'I also really liked the idea of making real objects of lasting quality, the practical link with use and home, and the large amount of technical knowledge required – enough to be interesting for an entire lifetime!'

Later moving to Sydney to undertake the full-time ceramics course at the National Art School in 1998, Tania mistakenly thought she would just learn how to throw and glaze, so that she could become a potter. 'But I had actually enrolled in a course with lots of drawing and art history, where I was challenged to consider ceramics as art. I have been negotiating a life somewhere between potter, artist, ceramicist and object-maker now for over eighteen years, and I am still addicted to clay.'

Drawing inspiration from 'everything she has ever seen', Tania finds it difficult to isolate a specific source. However, she includes nature, modernism,

Left: Nature is an important influence on Tania's work.

Scandinavian design, textiles, pattern, Indigenous Australian art, Japanese ceramics, her experiences growing up on a farm in Western Australia, studying graphic design, and living in the Southern Highlands of New South Wales as the most formative influences on her work. There is also a host of artists including Paul Klee, Joan Miró, Richard Tuttle, Philip Guston, Agnes Martin and Jürgen Partenheimer from whom she derives much creative stimulation.

Insisting that she is 'still trying to make something good', Tania is proud that she hasn't yet given up as many are tempted to do. She admits that her work is not terribly economically viable. 'I spend a ridiculous amount of time on individual works – both making and thinking time.' However, she feels very fortunate to have found good teaching jobs that ultimately finance her artistic freedom.

Tania says on the main challenges inherent in a career in clay is that ceramics provides opportunities for things to go wrong at every turn. While plenty of results that don't live up to initial expectations can be considered 'opportunities waiting to be realized' rather than failures, the disappointments are real. 'I regularly encounter cracks, glaze strangeness, colours disappearing during the firing, slip flaking off and pieces collapsing,' she says. 'Episodes of clumsiness – where I have knocked over and broken finished works while photographing them – are harder to swallow.'

CLAY

'My work combines mark making or drawing with ceramics. My signature would be a particular quality of line – a rather fragile, delicate line, which often contrasts with very simple, minimal forms.'

Above and opposite: Tania's work combines the immediate, ephemeral qualities of drawing and painting with the slower, more enduring aspects of clay.

Tara Burke

Above: Tara with one of her flower vases.

Tara Burke's interest in clay was first kindled when she was shopping for lovely handmade ceramics to give as a wedding gift. She was inspired to take a throwing class and later enrolled at Sydney College of the Arts. Despite pursuing a more formal education in ceramics, after a time Tania decided it wasn't for her and instead transferred into law at Sydney University.

At the same time as receiving her acceptance letter into law school, Tara was unexpectedly invited by a curator to participate in a group exhibition at a new Sydney gallery in January 2014, to show her burgeoning ceramics collection. Her pieces garnered more interest than she expected, promptly selling out on the opening day. Tara took this as a sign, propelling her into a more serious ceramics practice. 'Following my first show, it was the combination of many late nights, much support from the creative community, and a series of fortunate events that led me to where I am today. All up I've been practising for about four years – which equates to about a minute compared to some!' says Tara.

Deciding not to abandon law school but wanting to build a career in ceramics at the same time, Tara says the challenge has been trying to find a balance between the demand for her ceramics, her university studies and some personal time. She has had to learn the art of saying 'no' – an important skill to master!

Tara's work is organic and raw. Her signature handles seem to add an anthropomorphic element to her work which both charms and disarms people, making her pieces feel accessible. 'The handles are the bane of my existence some days, but I can't help it. They just make pieces more interesting,' she confesses.

Clay work is a slow and soothing process, which serves as a reminder to Tara that some things cannot be rushed. Almost all of her work is hand built. She employs a variety of stoneware and porcelain clays, and often creates her own clay combinations by recycling clay scraps, as well as foraging clays from greater New South Wales. 'I enjoy mixing clays as it provides a unique, unpredictable and usually very earthy result,' says Tara.

While surprises in ceramics can prove frustrating, if not heartbreaking, this is not always the case. 'Every now and then I open the kiln to the most magical and unexpected result. My kiln failed recently, which caused all of the work on the top shelf to over-fire. I opened the kiln to the most beautiful results – glazes that were totally burnt out in some parts but remained intact in others. I couldn't have caused those results intentionally, which is frustrating and somehow satisfying in equal parts. Sometimes you gotta just surrender to the kiln gods!'

Tara has developed a particular penchant for lustre firing. On one occasion, after inadvertently dropping a large and very expensive bottle of 18 carat gold lustre on the floor, she instinctively knew how to salvage the situation by turning a disaster into an opportunity. 'It's as if fight-or-flight mode kicked in and I knew I had to either cry or try to do something about it. I had a trophy-shaped vase sitting on my shelf, so I picked it up, and painted myself a shiny gold trophy,' she recalls. 'It's now my favourite piece!'

Above: The handles on Tara's vessels have become a signature of her work.

Above: Tara often makes use of gold lustre in her work.
Opposite: Almost all of Tara's work is hand built without the use of the wheel.

'I like to exploit the tactility of the material by contrasting raw and rough stoneware surfaces with smooth, pure white porcelains.'

Above and opposite: The natural environment is Tara's biggest influence, which is particularly evident in her use of texture.

Tessy King

Tessy King's work is immediately playful, colourful and lyrical. Some of her pieces are almost soft-looking and imperfect, while others are abstract forms with a sense of delicate rigidity. 'I focus largely on vessels for flowers, as I love making arrangements of these objects with flowers inside,' she says. For Tessy, ceramics is a way to express herself and understand a process that plays such an important role in the domestic environment.

All of Tessy's work is hand built using slab and coiling techniques. She tends to use porcelain paper clay for her slab forms and either porcelain or white stoneware for her coiled objects. She fires to stoneware temperature, or a little lower if she is concerned about the integrity of the piece. She either makes her own glazes or uses paint-on commercial glazes, depending on the object she is working with.

Tessy's distinctive style is influenced by the plethora of incidental details that she sees and hears around her. She draws inspiration from the internet, hard rubbish on the street, toys, kitsch objects from the 1980s and 1990s, textiles, her Ken Done duvet cover, orange gum blossoms, and listening to music by Townes Van Zandt on her iPod while she walks her dog. 'Lately though, my main inspiration comes from being outside in the intense Australian summer heat and light,' she says. 'I spend a lot of my spare time at one of the local swimming pools and the colours and sense of recreation are penetrating my work.' Given Tessy's love of working with colour – and her playful style – it is little wonder that she counts Betty Woodman's slab vessels and wall sculptures, and Beatrice Wood's iridescent pots among her inspirations.

Recalling a few forced experiences with clay in high school, Tessy admits that she didn't really take to the medium at that age. It wasn't until later, after taking a short wheel-throwing course at night, that she felt an affinity with clay. 'When I started art school I decided to focus on ceramics, as I wanted to build on the initial experiences that I had,' she says. 'I have always been interested in making things and understanding how things are made, and I feel it is this curiosity that pushed me to work with ceramics.' Art school was a very formative time for her practice. 'I loved it. I found that it pushed me conceptually and helped to quickly formulate a direction for my work. I did spend many extra hours in the studios experimenting, as it is such a great opportunity to use those facilities,' she says.

Working with clay is a messy, sometimes chaotic process. 'No matter how clean and uncluttered I make the studio, by the afternoon I am working surrounded by half-built objects, pots of underglaze colours, rolled out slabs and plastic bags of off-cuts,' Tessy admits. She believes that the environment helps her to be creative though. She also suggests that it's invaluable to be involved in a community of other makers, be they ceramicists or artists working in other mediums. 'Having the support and opportunity to work with other artists is exciting and leads to further connections,' she says.

'I have found that clay allows
me the opportunity to make
the objects that I want while
being spontaneous and playful
in my approach.'

Above and opposite: Tessy's work is inspired by the intense Australian summer heat and light, and the colours of her local swimming pool.

CLAY

Above and opposite: Tessy's work is hand built using slab and coiling techniques.

Thérèse Lebrun

Above: Thérèse examines one of her recent creations.

Thérèse Lebrun's work is informed by organic artefacts, recalling fossils or specimens collected from the beach – yet ultimately her pieces are articulations of her imagination. She creates shapes communicated around voids, which means her pieces are often extremely fragile and translucent. 'I push the porcelain to its limits, creating hidden places favourable to the emergence of dreams,' she describes.

Graduating from what used to be L'Académie des Arts et Métiers (now L'Académie Constantin Meunier) in Etterbeek, Brussels, in 1980, Thérèse has been practising professionally for thirty-six years – twelve of which have been focused on working with paper porcelain. Initially, she mostly produced thrown stoneware pieces covered with classical glazes such as tenmoku, celadon and copper red. While teaching ceramics, she began working with paper porcelain – a thin white material that turns translucent when fired – in order to be able to answer her students' technical questions. 'I have been fascinated by the results, and have kept working in this direction. Teaching has the interest of being a sharing of questions and exchanges, it is a stimulus that nourishes,' she explains. 'The presence of paper in the clay allows me to work on both dry or humid pieces. This property frees me of the time constraints and allows me to take it slow, which is an important thing in opposition to the current pace of life.'

Thérèse's process is very careful and considered, displaying an infinite patience. She starts with a collection of elements, mainly botanical; items that have lived and are not used anymore. These organic items are combined with paper porcelain, using the techniques of dipping and pouring. Thérèse then constructs her pieces by means of small repeated gestures, with elements clustered, assembled and reorganized so as to tell a new story. 'Recreating these universes in my own way, I compress time and materials, using basic elements such as water, earth, fire, air and plant matter. All of this leads me towards the creation of membranes, envelopes, skins, fossils, corals, phryganeae, cocoons – mysterious refuges for the worlds of our imagination,' she explains.

Thérèse's pieces are fired at 1280°C in a reduction atmosphere. The vegetal matter burns away, leaving hundreds of thin, semi-transparent clustered voids. Cast hollows are left by the bodies that have now disappeared. Thérèse's work poses the question of whether it is porcelain that structures the piece, or the tiny hollows to which the porcelain has given form.

Thérèse describes how her repetitive hand gestures create a certain meditative internal void. 'For me, ceramics is a popular and modest discipline. It is the oldest craft profession, a story that goes back to the earliest civilizations. By choosing this discipline, I am part of a lineage and participate in the transmission of knowledge and gestures. For me, ceramics is also working with a material that has its own life, its own history and that, therefore, is not easily tamed,' she muses.

Thérèse is delighted by the current surge of interest in ceramics. 'It is interesting to notice that – at last – one speaks of ceramics in the world of contemporary art,' she says.

Above: Thérèse surrounds herself with nature, and its influence is evident in her work.

Above and opposite: Thérèse's works take their shape from the organic elements she uses to make them.

'My way of creating
begins with doing,
rather than thinking.'

Tracy Muirhead

Tracy Muirhead says that she doesn't have a ceramics muse, and consciously tries to avoid looking at what others do in order to remain true to herself. 'However, I acknowledge the zeitgeist effect, and also that sadly nothing is new in art, so have learnt to get over my ego!' she says.

What Tracy strives to achieve with her practice is to present a piece of the Earth in a different, yet honest, form, highlighting the beauty inherent in the natural clay. 'I aim to manipulate it as little as possible and allow the clay to present itself by finding the form within – then the trick is to figure out how to reproduce it,' she states. 'I am most influenced by shapes and the appreciation of beauty in the imperfect and wobbly, which is discovered by a sense of exploration and a desire to uncover what is presented.'

Born in South Africa, Tracy's path to ceramics was a convoluted one. Despite a love of making things in her youth, she studied psychology at university, then pursued a career as a fashion buyer. Eventually migrating to Australia in 1998 with her family, her focus was then on raising two children. 'In 2005 a good friend suggested pottery classes to fill the time after our youngest started school, and little did I know it would become a major part of my life. I was immediately hooked – although the first task of making a pinch-pot bird looked nothing like a bird! I was obsessed with my newfound creative outlet and quickly became prolific,' explains Tracy.

Her interest in ceramics subsequently became more serious and Tracy studied part-time for four years, graduating in 2010. 'After which I floated around trying to figure out how to enter the market. I am ever grateful to Judith Buckeridge from Potier in Melbourne for believing in me and stocking my pots in her beautiful ceramics store for the past five years,' she says.

Tracy's work is best described as sculptural functional ware, and her style is simple, pared back and organic. Many of her pieces are reminiscent of African and Japanese pots. They are predominantly hand built using a variety of stoneware clays, including porcelaneous white clay from Australia, black clay from the UK, terracotta and groggy clays. 'Most of my work is slab built and either rolled as thinly as possible using a large rolling pin, or chunks of solid clay taken straight from the block. I tend to push clay to the extremes – thin and fragile or thick, chunky, solid pieces that could potentially blow up in the kiln,' she details.

Left: Tracy's pieces are pared
back and functional, but with
a sculptural quality.

'The most heartbreaking disaster occurred early on in my play with clay. I was told I couldn't fire solid pieces so I just had to try and find a way – call me stubborn or persistent. One of my solid balls blew up in a communal kiln and destroyed a child's work. That really devastated me, but also galvanized my desire to further my education in ceramics.'

Patience is Tracy's biggest challenge. Her kiln takes two days to heat up and cool down, and each piece is first bisque fired, then has glaze applied and is glaze fired. 'Four days of firing can be rather taxing on your patience!' she admits.

What brings Tracy the most pleasure is seeing her pieces in situ – either on a benchtop or on a table – enhancing daily rituals. 'I love seeing how one pot can interact with another and create a statement prior to being put to use.'

Her advice to students looking to follow in her footsteps is to always test new things. 'Don't copy yourself. Keep your eyes and mind open to everything – shapes, colour and textures,' she says. 'Also keep a record of what you did and how you did it, with photographic reference. Write things down in a visual diary and never assume you'll remember everything – you may want to revisit something years later. Be open-minded and accept each piece as a unique expression.'

Above and opposite: Tracy aims to reproduce the natural shapes of the earth in her work, appreciating the beauty of the imperfect.

'My aim is to make pots
that make us stop for
a moment, be present
and reflect.'

Ulrica Trulsson

What Ulrica Trulsson hopes to capture in her work is a sense of exploration and discovery, and a love for making and the processes involved. 'There is quite a clear reference to the earth and landscape in my work in general, and I want to evoke that same revelation of interesting details and unexpected finds,' she explains.

Ulrica sees everyday utilitarian objects as complex and purposeful, and their forms, although archetypal, have endless possible resolutions. Her approach is exploratory, allowing her to spend time finding her own personal interpretation.

The urge to explore has been formative for Ulrica, who was born and raised in Sweden, left in her teens to spend time in Scotland, then started a new life in Australia. These geographical shifts have ultimately fed her artistic expression. She always believed she would be a creative practitioner one day and, when she undertook pottery short courses in Melbourne in 2009, she knew ceramics would be her future. Ulrica undertook a two-year Diploma of Ceramics, and her teachers provided a wonderful foundation from which to build her own practice. Ulrica relocated to Adelaide in 2012 to take part in the JamFactory's renowned Associate Training Program.

'During my time in the program I was surrounded by inspiring, dedicated practitioners on a daily basis.

As an emerging artist it was invaluable to have the input of the staff, tenants and other associates,' she recalls. 'I was lucky enough to have mentors like esteemed ceramicists Kirsten Coelho and Prue Venables. Taking part in the associate program gave me the opportunity to reflect on my practice and focus on how to develop and perfect my work. Since completing the training program in 2013, I have been a studio tenant at JamFactory.'

There is an apparent simplicity to Ulrica's aesthetic, which is underpinned by detailing in the making – from the fitting of lids and the structure of knobs and handles, to the assembling of pots made from several components, such as teapots or jugs with thrown and altered components.

Ulrica says that she sees pots in her imagination and gets excited to bring them to life. Enduring sources of inspiration are striations in rocks, patterns found on pebbles and stones, and surfaces formed by water over time. 'Another inspiration has been snow and the way it transforms the landscape and everyday things, such as the way it accumulates on rooftops, letterboxes and lamp posts. I believe these "chosen" sources of inspiration are just one part of a jigsaw of impressions and catalysts for ideas in everyday life,' she elaborates.

Left: Ulrica uses a combination of wheel throwing and hand building to constantly push her skills and craftsmanship.

Ulrica uses various stoneware clay bodies, at times mixed or marbled on the wheel, contrasting with or complementing each other. She also varies her glazes and her firing method. Gas reduction firing and oxidation firing help to bring out the qualities of different materials.

'Mostly I work with satin glaze surfaces. They are beautiful to touch and invite the objects to be picked up and handled. I also work with very thin layers of glaze where the roughness of iron-rich reduction-fired stoneware clays creates yet another effect. I leave some work or areas of work unglazed, to emphasise the beauty of the clays,' Ulrica explains.

The process of wheel throwing is central to Ulrica's practice, however she combines this with hand-building techniques, striving to continually stretch and perfect her craftsmanship. 'It makes me excited to think how this will allow my work to develop over time,' she says.

There are two concurrent strains to Ulrica's work – production and exhibition – and she admits that it can be a challenge to find the time to realize the hopes and dreams that she has for both facets of her work. But she does concede that being a full-time maker means she is fortunate enough to explore the medium and turn her practice into whatever she wants it to be. 'Each new pot I make gives me ideas for so many more, and I get to keep discovering what I can make. I feel fulfilled knowing I am pursuing my passion.'

Above and opposite: Ulrica's aesthetic is simple but her work stands out through its details, such as the fitting of lids or the patterns used.

'My stoneware pots celebrate the materials I use, and each pot has its own subtle peculiarities.'

CLAY

Above: Ulrica uses a range of stoneware clay bodies, sometimes marbling them on the wheel.
Opposite: Texture is important in Ulrica's work, and she wants to make pieces that invite people to pick them up and handle them.

Valerie Restarick

Henri Matisse once stated, 'Creativity takes courage'. Valerie Restarick adds, 'People working in clay are some of the bravest.' Something of a veteran of the ceramics scene, Valerie has a good thirty years in the studio under her belt. Originally trained as a painter at the National Gallery Art School in Melbourne, she always felt she had a stronger affinity for clay. Straight after her studies, she left Australia to teach art in London and, while there, took pottery classes by night. 'I very quickly became addicted,' she recalls.

Although Valerie has many ceramic inspirations, it's mainly the British craft movements of the 20th century and their response to the Japanese studio pottery aesthetic that have influenced her work. While she admits to having had various muses over the years, Valerie finds herself always going back to the ceramicists Sandy Lockwood and Takeshi Yasuda.

Having worked in many different pottery studios early on in her career, Valerie opened a purpose-built studio within her home almost two decades ago. This was a pivotal event in her life, allowing her to be completely immersed in her practice and further blurring her life and work boundaries.

Valerie describes her style as spontaneous and instinctive. She tends to be a chameleon with her ideas, using art at times to express her political and environmental beliefs and passions. Her other stream, wheel-thrown functional ware, emphasises the purity of form over decorative details. 'I like the challenge of using clay to express my ideas. It's hard to direct the results. There are so many other elements at play and the final piece can be surprising – either enlightening or greatly disappointing.'

Despite her vast experience, there's no end of things to learn. Most recently for Valerie this has taken the form of raku: 'Scary, frightening, dangerous. It's always a challenge when learning and adapting new ceramic techniques to your ideas,' she admits.

Similarly, as with many artists across various creative fields, there is the contentious issue of commissions. 'It's always hard to completely satisfy what the client wants. Often the clients don't fully understand the limitations of production, or that it can be difficult and a lengthy process,' Valerie concedes.

To the up-and-coming generation of potters, Valerie's advice is very simple: 'Find an artist you admire and pester them! Having a mentor to work for and with is rewarding for the student and the teacher alike,' she enthuses.

Valerie sees the current renaissance in ceramics as part of a larger movement in handmade products, one that she hopes will continue to develop and expand into other areas too.

Previous page: Valerie at work in her purpose-built studio.
Above: Valerie uses ceramics as an outlet to express her personal and political views.
Opposite: Valerie's work emphasises the purity of form over decoration.

'I was – and still am – seduced by the immediacy of clay. It's a tactile material that responds directly to your hands. Forms just come into their own.'

Vipoo Srivilasa

Vipoo Srivilasa has been working as a full-time artist for almost twenty years. His first ceramic experience was at the College of Fine Arts in Thailand where it was not love at first sight, but more of a slow-burn kind of relationship. 'As time went on I slowly grew to love ceramics,' he says.

His true development as a professional artist began when Vipoo moved to Australia in 1997 to undertake a Master of Fine Art and Design (Ceramics) at the University of Tasmania, where he was later offered an Honorary Research Associate position. Now living in Melbourne, Vipoo works predominantly in ceramics and enjoys creating work that interacts with audiences or involves the community. 'I'm also beginning to expand my practice by incorporating other art forms and media into my ceramic work,' he says.

While he does enjoy painting and drawing, canvas has never held the same appeal for Vipoo. He always ends up painting on clay, which he describes as an 'addictive material'. Porcelain is his preferred medium, and his technique of choice is hand building. Vipoo finds this very satisfying, as he loves to do anything that requires working with his hands.

At first glance, Vipoo's work appears to be whimsical and playful, but his expressively painted ceramic vessels, figurines and sculptures are intrinsically connected to his bicultural experiences. Choosing to borrow a friend's words, Vipoo describes his work as a 'playful blend of historical, figurative and decorative art practices with a healthy dose of contemporary culture'.

Vipoo's pieces are highly collectible, and he's exhibited widely throughout Australia and internationally in high-profile galleries and private collections. As an artist, Vipoo has gone on to receive wide recognition for his meticulous works.

Despite the acclaim, Vipoo does offer some comfort to his fellow ceramicists, admitting that even he is prone to the odd disaster — such as finishing complicated pieces only to realize after firing that he had used the wrong clay.

To the next generation of ceramicists, Vipoo's advice is wise. 'Write all your ideas, projects and tasks down and then prioritize them in order of urgency. Learn the art of saying no, as there are times when there are too many good opportunities and you just can't take them all. And network like crazy, both in and outside the ceramics world.'

Left: Vipoo's work draws on a wide range
of decorative art practices.
Following pages: Vipoo's work displays the
influence of his Thai and Australian cultures.

'I love experimenting, using clay as an interactive medium and developing my work into relational art.'

Glossary

ANAGAMA KILN. An ancient Japanese style of wood-fired pottery kiln.

BALL CLAY. A popular sedimentary clay, which is fine-grained and plastic in nature, producing a white-coloured pottery body when fired.

BAND. Lines marked around circular ceramic objects using decorative methods and tools. The act of marking a band is called 'banding'.

BISCUIT/BISQUE. Pottery that has been fired but not yet glazed. 'Biscuit firing' or 'bisque firing' is the preliminary firing prior to glazing.

BODY. The structural part of a ceramic object.

BONE CHINA. Glass-like, translucent pottery made from a body of the following approximate composition: 45–50 per cent calcined bone, 20–25 per cent kaolin and 25–30 per cent china stone.

BONE DRY. The final stage of greenware when it is in a completely dry state and ready to be fired. In this stage, the clay is very fragile, non-plastic and porous.

CARBONIZING. The introduction of carbon particles during firing to cause the permanent staining of a ceramic material.

CELADON. Glazes containing iron, which produce green, grey and grey–blue colours in reduction firing.

CHINA CLAY. See: kaolin.

CHUCK. A piece used to aid the potter in trimming. A chuck is a form that can hold a pot upside-down above the wheel head while the potter trims. Chucks are thrown and bisque-fired clay cylinders which are open on both sides.

CLAY. Widely occurring aluminum silicate mineral resulting from natural decomposition of feldspar and granite. Composed of microscopic disc-shaped platelets that give clay its slippery, plastic quality.

CLAY BODY. The clay mixture used to form ceramic and pottery objects. Often made up of different types of clay.

COILING. A hand-building method of forming pottery by building up the walls with coils of rope-like rolls.

CRACKLE GLAZE. A glaze that develops fine, web-like cracks in the surface.

CRAWLING. A fault in a ceramics glaze causing it to recede away from an object during the firing and leaving areas of unglazed clay. It is also used intentionally in controlled crawl glazing.

CRYSTAL GLAZE. A glaze that forms crystals upon cooling.

DE-AIRING. To remove air from clay via a vacuum apparatus, making the clay denser and more plastic.

DELFTWARE. Tin-glazed earthenware, usually white with blue hand-formed decorative motifs.

DIPPING. Applying a glaze or slip to a pottery item by immersing it and then shaking off excess glaze.

DUNT. A crack caused by thermal shock, which occurs if a pot cools too quickly after firing.

EARTHENWARE. Pottery created by low-temperature firing.

ENGOBE. A coating of white or coloured slip, which can be applied to an article to improve its appearance – to give a smoother surface to a rough body, to mask an inferior colour or for decorative effect. Slips or engobes can also be applied using painting techniques, and can be used in isolation or in several layers and colours.

FIRING. The process of heating pottery in a kiln to bring the glaze or clay body to maturity – and to make the clay reach its maximum non-porosity and hardness.

FLASHING SLIP. Slip that is painted or dipped onto wares in order to promote flashing effects in the firing.

FLATWARE. Relatively flat items of crockery such as plates and saucers.

FLUX. The melting agent in a glaze.

FOOT. The base of a ceramic form, often a ring.

FUSION. Occurs during the firing of pottery when the clay and glaze surfaces combine to create a thin layer made up of the two materials.

GLAZE. A vitreous coating bonded to a ceramic by heat.

GLAZE FIRING. The firing stage during which the glaze materials melt and form a vitreous coating on the surface of the clay article.

GREENWARE. Unfired pottery.

GROG. A ceramic raw material with a high percentage of silica and alumina. Grog can be produced by firing selected fire clays to high temperature, then grinding and screening to specific particle sizes. The particle-size distribution is generally coarser than other raw materials used to prepare clay bodies. Grog tends to be porous and low-density, and is normally available as a powder or as chippings.

HAGI. Originating in Korea, a high-fired stoneware notable for its white-glazed teaware.

IKEBANA. The Japanese art of flower arrangement.

IRON OXIDE. A common oxide in glazes and some clays, generally imparting a reddish-brown colour.

JIGGER. A machine for forming ceramic plates or other flatware from clay in a mould rotating beneath a template.

JOLLEY. A machine for forming cups, bowls and other hollowware from clay in a mould rotating beneath a template.

KAOLIN. A white firing clay used to make porcelain.

KASAMA. A Japanese city famous for its ceramics known as 'Kasama ware'. Kasama produces various types of clay that have high granite contents. The clays are rich in plasticity and contain a lot of iron, so they turn brown after firing.

KIDNEY. A kidney-shaped tool used for finishing thrown pots as well as smoothing clay in a mould.

KILN. A furnace for firing ceramics.

KINTSUGI. The Japanese art of repairing broken ceramics with lacquer dusted or mixed with powdered gold, silver or platinum.

KNEADING. Working clay on a surface with the palms of the hands in order to remove air from it and obtain a uniform consistency, so the clay is ready to be shaped.

KOHIKI WARE. High-fired ware with a white surface that is achieved by covering clay with slip.

LEATHER HARD. The damp but stiffened stage in the drying of clay.

LUSTRE. A material applied to and fired on glazed earthenware to produce decorative metallic tints.

LUSTRE FIRING. The process of firing glazed earthenware at low temperature after the application of the lustre material.

LUTING. A method of joining together two pieces of dry or leather-hard clay using slip.

MAJOLICA. A low-fire glazing technique first developed in Majorca. The process involves applying an opaque tin glaze to earthenware and painting it with coloured oxides.

MATTE GLAZE. A dull-surfaced glaze with no gloss.

MENTORI. A method of oriental influence that alters the surface of a soft clay object by cutting off slices that can vary in size, to form many sides or facets.

NERIKOMI. The use of two or more contrasting clay colours to throw or hand build pottery. Coloured clays are wedged together becoming marbled, and then thrown on the pottery wheel or hand built into forms.

NUKA. A type of ash glaze commonly used in Karatsu ware, kohiki ware and white hagi ware.

OXBLOOD. Also known as sang de boeuf or flambé glaze, this is a glossy, blood red glaze commonly slashed with streaks of purple or turquoise. Often used to decorate porcelain.

OXIDATION. Firing with a full supply of oxygen so that the metals in the clay and glaze produce their bright oxide colours. Electric kilns fire in oxidation.

PAPER CLAY. Ordinary plastic clay mixed with up to 50 per cent reconstituted paper pulp. Paper greatly strengthens the unfired clay, making this a preferred material for hand builders and sculptors.

PINCHING. A hand-building method where objects are formed by pinching clay repeatedly between thumb and fingers, or between the fingers of one hand and the palm of the opposing hand.

PINHOLES. Faults in the surface of a ceramic form that appear as small holes in the glazed surface, caused by escaping gases.

PLASTICITY. The quality of clay that allows it to be manipulated and maintain its shape without cracking.

PORCELAIN. High-fired vitreous clay body containing kaolin, silica, fluxes and often ball clay to increase plasticity, with a total clay component of no more than 50 per cent. Usually pure white, some porcelains may fire translucent when thin.

POTTERY. Items made of fired clay – broadly divided into earthenware, porcelain and stoneware.

PYROMETRIC CONES. A device designed to measure high temperatures, consisting of a series of cones that melt at different temperatures.

RAKU. A process by which pottery is fired at a relatively low temperature and then moved while hot to a closed container holding combustible materials (such as sawdust) which ignite and react with the pottery's surface, resulting in colours and patterns.

RAW GLAZING. Glazing greenware for single firing.

REDUCTION. Firing in a low-oxygen kiln to achieve certain colours.

SGRAFFITO. A form of decoration made by scratching through a surface to reveal a lower layer of contrasting colour, typically done in slip on ceramics before firing.

SHINO. A thick frost-like glaze made from nearly 100 per cent rock-forming mineral feldspar. Colours range from white to orange with occasional charcoal-coloured flecks.

SHINOGI. A Japanese decorative technique that involves hand-carving a fluted pattern in the surface of a ceramic form; often executed in contrasting black and white.

SHIVERING. A severe glaze problem that occurs when a glaze is under too much compression. The fired glaze looks like paint peeling off the underlying clay body.

SINGLE FIRED. In most cases pottery is fired multiple times – first focusing on form, and then decoration. Some ceramicists prefer to single fire, combining the bisque and glaze firings as they feel it achieves a better clay–glaze interface.

SLAB. Flat sections of clay created by pressing or rolling; used in hand building.

SLIP. A clay in liquid suspension used decoratively or as a binding agent. Clay slips often have oxides added to them for decorative purposes.

SLURRY. Slurry is an aqueous suspension of clay and water. Similar to slip, but with a thicker consistency.

SOAKING. Holding the kiln at a steady temperature during firing to allow proper formation of some clay and glaze effects. The period of time the kiln is held at temperature depends on the effect the potter wishes to achieve.

SODA FIRING. An atmospheric firing technique where sodium bicarbonate or sodium carbonate is introduced into the kiln when it has almost reached peak temperature (usually 2350°C). This gives rise to organic patterns of colour and dimpling. The resulting colours can be a range of oranges with yellow and red tones, rich browns, golds and tans.

STAIN. Ceramic colourants that have been fused together to eliminate solubility problems, resulting in greater stability in firing and truer colour representation prior to firing.

STONEWARE. Hard and durable vitreous wares produced at high temperatures. Non-porous.

TENMOKUS. A dark glaze with a surface that resembles oil spotting; found in Chinese and Japanese ceramics.

TERRACOTTA. A brownish-red hard-fired clay.

TERRA SIGILLATA. Ultra-refined clay slip that can give a soft sheen when applied to bone-dry wares, and a high gloss finish if polished or burnished while still damp. The Ancient Greeks and Romans used this technique instead of glaze.

THERMAL SHOCK. Occurs when too much stress is created in a piece of pottery or ceramic during the heating and cooling process. It comes from temperature differences in the piece and can cause small to large cracks, or the piece may actually break.

THROWING. Forming or shaping on a potter's wheel.

UNDERGLAZE. Decoration applied to biscuit pottery before it is covered with a glaze.

VITREOUS. Glass-like; pertaining to the hard finish of a fired glaze, or the non-absorbency of a fired body.

WABI-SABI. A Japanese tradition of aesthetics and philosophy that embraces transience and imperfection. In ceramics, the style is often expressed as rustic and simple-looking functional pieces.

WEDGING. A procedure for preparing clay, which involves mixing and de-airing clay by cutting it diagonally and vigorously working the pieces together.

WHEEL. A device with either a manual (foot-powered) or electric rotating wheel on which a potter shapes round ceramic forms. See also: Throwing.

ZOGAN. A technique of inlaying slip, underglaze or clay into a contrasting clay body, which allows for intricate design work in ceramics.

Photography Credits

2: Clare Plueckhahn; 8, 9: Luisa Brimble; 10–13: Toshiko Hirai; 15–19: Tsutsumi Yano; 21, 22: Alana Wilson; 23: Simone Gooch; 25: Kern Hendricks; 26: Mim Stirling; 27: Matthew Stanton; 29, 30: Sabine Bannard; 31–33: Alan Benson; 35–37: Clare Plueckhahn; 38: Felix Odell; 39–41: Patric Johansson; 44–47: Anna-Karina Elias; 49: Sue Hanna; 50, 51: Sylvain Deleu; 51–55: Vanessa Champion; 57–61: Cécile Daladier; 62–65: Brett Stewart; 67–69: Allister Payne; 71–73: Christopher Martin; 75–77: Florian Gadsby; 79: Jane Beiles; 80, 81: Frances Palmer; 83–87 Georgia Harvey; 89–91: Giselle Hicks; 93–95: Dirk Theys; 96–99: Victoria May Harrison; 101: Parker Blain; 102: Document Photography; 103: Parker Blain; 104–107: Jeremy Simons; 109–111: Annie Portelli; 113–116: Jono Smart; 117: Charlotte Fletcher; 119, 120: Ashley Mackevicius; 121: Julie Pennington; 122–125: Andre Castellucci; 127, 128: Katie Jacobs; 129: Stuart Brown; 130–133: Greg Piper; 135–137: Kira Ni Ceramics; 139–143: Linda Lopez; 144: Lucile Sciallano; 145: Luisa Brimble; 146, 147: Lucile Sciallano; 149: Lynda Draper; 150: Mark Draper; 151–153: Lynda Draper; 155–157: Docqment; 158, 159: Joy Lai and John Dennis; 161: Lucy Browning; 162: Maria de Hann; 163: Jonathan Gooch; 165–167: Maryam Riazi; 169–171: Amy Piddington; 173–177: Aya Sekine; 179–181: Oded Antman; 182–186: Teagan Glenane; 188–191: Carlos Avendaño; 192–197: Shantanu Starick; 199–201: Tatiana C Scott; 202–205: Ole Akhoe; 207: Charlie McKay; 208, 209: Mariell Amélie; 211: Sabrina Talarico; 212, 213: Chris Sanders; 215: Zoe O'Donnell Photography; 216, 217: Tania Rollond; 218–223: Luisa Brimble; 225: Zara Poole; 226: Tessy King; 227: Lauren Bamford; 228, 229: Zara Poole; 230–233: Paul Gruszow; 235–237: Andrew Barcham; 239: Tom Roschi; 240, 241: Grant Hancock; 242, 243: Josie Withers; 245–247: Rebecca Newman Photography; 249, 250: Korakij Chaisirisopo; 251: Andrew Barcham.

Artwork Credits

DAWN VACHON. p68, top: *Sugar Block and Buttress*, 2016. Clay, glaze, stained feldspar. p68, bottom: *F/Wall and Lolli-prop*, 2016. Clay, glaze.

HOLLY MACDONALD. p102: *Bouteille à la mer III*, 2015. Australian porcelain, porcelain slip, iron oxide, ceramic stain, ceramic pencil.

KATIE JACOBS. p127: *Kangaroo Pourer* and *Birch Tree Vases*.

LYNDA DRAPER. p149: *Self Portrait with Hair Down*, 2015. Hand built, earthenware and glaze. p150: *Mary Mary*, 2015. Hand built, earthenware and glaze. p151: *Pearly King*, 2015. Hand built, earthenware and glaze. p152: *Tiara*, 2015. Hand built, earthenware and majolica glaze. (top) p153: *Genie Bottle*, 2015. Earthenware.

MADELEINE PRESTON. p156, top: *Celadon, Blue and Baby Pink Trophies* (installation view), 2015. p156, bottom: *Yellow Shell Dish*, 2015. p157: *Overfired and Overtired*, 2015.

SEAN GERSTLEY. p188: *Little Lemon Vase*, 2015. Ceramic. p189: *Easy G, Draft Dodger* and *Paint Can*, 2014. Ceramic. p190: *Song Cry*, 2014. Ceramic. p191: *Sitting In A Diner*, 2014. Ceramic.

STEEN IPSEN. p203: *Tied-Up 12-12*, 2012. Blue glazed earthenware with pink PVC. p204: *Organic 1-15*, 2015. White glazed earthenware decorated with decal paper. p205, top: *Organic 2-14*, 2015. White glazed earthenware decorated with decal paper. p205, bottom: *Organic 3-13*, 2013. White glazed earthenware decorated with decal paper.

TESSY KING. p225: *Ikebana Object*, 2014. Porcelain. p226, top: *Sand*, 2015. Porcelain raku terracotta. p226, bottom: *Hot Days Outside*, 2015. Porcelain. p227: *My Heart is a Yellow Room* (installation view), 2015. Mixed media.

VIPOO SRIVILASA. p249: *The Saver*, 2015. Clay, glaze and gold lustre. p250: *Aliens Goddess*, 2015. p251: *Happy Land* series, 2015. Cobalt pigment on porcelain, mixed media and gold lustre.

Contact Details

AKIKO HIRAI COLLINGWOOD	akikohiraiceramics.com	KEIKO MATSUI	keikomatsui.com.au
AKIO NUKAGA	akio-nukaga.com	KIRA NI	kirani.co
ALANA WILSON	alanawilson.com	LINDA LOPEZ	lindalopez.net
ALEXANDRA STANDEN	alexandrastanden.com	LUCILE SCIALLANO	apetitefabriquedebrunswick.com
ALISON FRASER	slabandslub.com.au	LYNDA DRAPER	lyndadraper.com
ANDREI DAVIDOFF	andreidavidoff.com	MADELEINE PRESTON	madeleinepreston.com.au
ANNA-KARINA	-	MARIA DE HAAN	mariadehaan.com
ANNA LERINDER	lerinder.se	MARYAM RIAZI	maryamriazi.com/clay
ASHRAF HANNA	ashrafhanna.net	MILLY DENT	millydent.com
BRIGITTE COLLEAUX	poterie-brigittecolleaux.co.uk	MIZUYO YAMASHITA	mizuyo.com
CÉCILE DALADIER	ceciledaladier.com	RACHEL BOXNBOIM	rachelboxnboim.com
CLAIRE JOHNSON	-	RUBY PILVEN	rubypilven.com
DAWN VACHON	dawnvachon.com	SEAN GERSTLEY	seangerstley.com
DEREK WILSON	derekwilsonceramics.com	SOPHIE HARLE	-
FLORIAN GADSBY	floriangadsby.com	SOPHIE MORAN	sophiemoran.info
FRANCES PALMER	francespalmerpottery.com	STEEN IPSEN	steen-ipsen.dk
GEORGIA HARVEY	georgiaharvey.net	STINE DULONG	skandihus.co.uk
GISELLE HICKS	gisellehicks.com	SUSAN ROBEY	susanrobeyceramics.com
GUY VAN LEEMPUT	guyvanleemput.be	TANIA ROLLOND	taniarollond.com
HANNAH LAWRENCE	hannahlawrence.net	TARA BURKE	taraburkeceramics.com
HOLLY MACDONALD	holly-macdonald.com	THÉRÈSE LEBRUN	-
JEREMY SIMONS	slipceramics.com	TESSY KING	tessymking.tumblr.com
JESSILLA ROGERS	jessillarogers.com	TRACY MUIRHEAD	tracymuirhead.com
JONO SMART	jonosmart.co.uk	ULRICA TRULSSON	ulricatrulsson.com
JULIE PENNINGTON	juliepenningtonceramics.net	VALERIE RESTARICK	valerierestarick.com
KATIA CARLETTI	katiacarletti.com	VIPOO SRIVILASA	vipoo.com
KATIE JACOBS	katiejacobs.net		

ACKNOWLEDGMENTS

Abundant gratitude must go to Thames & Hudson, in particular to Paulina de Laveaux, for providing an opportunity to immerse myself in what can only be described as a dream project. Thank you to all the excessively clever ceramicist friends in my midst who in recent years have been instrumental in whetting my appetite for clay, and have educated and enthused me more than they realize.

I am in awe of the ceramic artists who contributed to this book, who took time away from their studios (where I know they really wanted to be!) to indulge me and my prying questions – and for answering so authentically. To the clever Ngaio Parr, who designed this beautiful book and as usual exceeded the bounds of my imagination – thank you.

Thanks to my family for allowing me to be so distracted! And a special thank you must go to my third-born baby Ash, who held off being born while I completed the book. Almost.